UNDERSTANDING
FOUR VIEWS
ON BAPTISM

Books in the Counterpoints Series

Church Life

Bible and Theology

UNDERSTANDING FOUR VIEWS ON BAPTISM

- **Thomas J. Nettles**
- **Richard L. Pratt Jr.**
- **Robert Kolb**
- **John D. Castelein**

- **John H. Armstrong** *general editor*
- **Paul E. Engle** *series editor*

ZONDERVAN.com/
AUTHORTRACKER
follow your favorite authors

ZONDERVAN

Understanding Four Views on Baptism
Copyright © 2007 by John H. Armstrong

Requests for information should be addressed to:

Zondervan, *Grand Rapids, Michigan 49530*

Library of Congress Cataloging-in-Publication Data

Nettles, Tom J.
    Understanding four views on baptism / Thomas J. Nettles, Richard L. Pratt Jr.,
    Robert Kolb.
        p. cm. — (Counterpoints)
    Includes bibliographical references and indexes.
    ISBN 978-0-310-26267-1
    1. Baptism — History of doctrines.   I. Pratt, Richards L., 1953-   II. Kolb, Robert.
III. Title.
BV811.3.N48 2006
234'.161 — dc22

                                                                        2006026525

Printed in the United States of America

11 12 13 14 15 16 • 24 23 22 21 20 19 18 17 16 15 14 13 12 11 10 9 8 7 6

CONTENTS

ABBREVIATIONS

BIBLE TEXTS, VERSIONS, ETC.

KJV	King James Version
NASB	New American Standard Bible
NIV	New International Version
NRSV	New Revised Standard Version
NT	New Testament
OT	Old Testament

OLD TESTAMENT, NEW TESTAMENT

Gen.	Genesis
Exod.	Exodus
Lev.	Leviticus
Num.	Numbers
Deut.	Deuteronomy
Josh.	Joshua
Judg.	Judges
Ruth	Ruth
1–2 Sam.	1–2 Samuel
1–2 Kgs.	1–2 Kings
1–2 Chr.	1–2 Chronicles
Ezra	Ezra
Neh.	Nehemiah
Esth.	Esther
Job	Job
Ps./Pss.	Psalm/Psalms
Prov.	Proverbs
Eccl.	Ecclesiastes
Song	Song of Songs
Isa.	Isaiah

Jer.	Jeremiah
Lam.	Lamentations
Ezek.	Ezekiel
Dan.	Daniel
Hos.	Hosea
Joel	Joel
Amos	Amos
Obad.	Obadiah
Jonah	Jonah
Mic.	Micah
Nah.	Nahum
Hab.	Habakkuk
Zeph.	Zephaniah
Hag.	Haggai
Zech.	Zechariah
Mal.	Malachi
Matt.	Matthew
Mark	Mark
Luke	Luke
John	John
Acts	Acts
Rom.	Romans
1–2 Cor.	1–2 Corinthians
Gal.	Galatians
Eph.	Ephesians
Phil.	Philippians
Col.	Colossians
1–2 Thess.	1–2 Thessalonians
1–2 Tim.	1–2 Timothy
Titus	Titus
Phlm.	Philemon
Heb.	Hebrews
Jas.	James
1–2 Pet.	1–2 Peter
1–2–3 John	1–2–3 John
Jude	Jude
Rev.	Revelation

GENERAL

AD	*anno Domini* (in the year of [our] Lord)
BC	before Christ
ca.	*circa* (around, about, approximately)
cf.	*confer*, compare
ed(s).	editor(s), edited by
e.g.	*exempli gratia*, for example
ibid.	*ibidem*, in the same place
i.e.	*id est*, that is
n.	note
p(p).	page(s)
v(v).	verse(s)

INTRODUCTION: DIVISION, DIFFERENCES, AND A DREAM

John H. Armstrong

Most Christians agree that baptism is important. In fact, the overwhelming majority of Christians believe that it is very important. Didn't Jesus himself submit to baptism? And didn't Jesus clearly command it for his followers? Furthermore, didn't the apostles and the leaders of the early church baptize those who came to faith in Jesus of Nazareth?

The NT abounds with clear evidence that baptism mattered to early Christians. And the history of the Christian church for nearly two thousand years demonstrates that baptism has always mattered to Christians in all ages and all contexts. One conclusion we cannot draw, at least from the Bible or church history, is that we can treat baptism as unimportant.

THE DIFFICULTY

Let's face it, nothing more quickly leads to disagreement among otherwise agreeable Christians than a discussion about the meaning and method (mode) of Christian baptism. There are almost as many reasons for disagreement about baptism as there are views and positions held by Christians on baptism.

But the most basic questions remain: What is the real significance of baptism? How does God work in this act? What does it mean to receive Christian baptism? And is baptism necessary for salvation? As if these questions weren't vexing enough, we have the added difficulty of deciding who should be baptized. Should we baptize only those who can profess faith through a clear understanding of the gospel and desire publicly to express a personal commitment to Jesus? What about the children of Christian parents, particularly infants who cannot answer questions about faith? Put another way, what should the church give to the children of faithful parents who desire to give their offspring all that God provides for such children? And if these two questions aren't difficult enough, there is a third one regarding the mode of baptism. Should we immerse in water the person being baptized, or is it enough to sprinkle or pour water over them? Does it even matter?

Let's be very clear at the outset. There are godly, faithful, and earnest students of the Bible who hold to different views about water baptism. Disagreement about baptism is not proof of rebellion, stupidity, or immaturity. Some of the most wonderful Christians you and I know fail to agree with one another about baptism. This is water that really does divide real Christians.[1]

I have formed a few ideas about why we differ on this subject. Some of my ideas are merely opinions about the nature of disagreement in general; others are views I've formed based on how I have come to understand the Bible. There is one thing I am quite sure about, after many years of wrestling with this issue: Christians who do not agree with me are not better or worse than I am because of their understanding of baptism. Their love for Jesus and his love for them is not somehow inferior to my love for Jesus or his love for me simply because we do not agree about baptism.

We must nevertheless face the fact that this issue does divide us. Seeking to ignore the problem will not solve it. We can, and we must, work at overcoming the disagreements we can overcome. We can, and we must, remove prejudices and fears wherever possible. And we should seek to understand why we disagree and thus learn how to face our disagreements with a better knowledge of real differences. All the while we must dig deep into Scripture and church tradition, seeking to understand why we believe what we do and what these beliefs mean for our own lives of faith. In the end, "to his own master [each person] stands or falls" (Rom. 14:4).

One more word is in order regarding our differences over baptism. We must all realize that we are finite beings. None of us will ever be able to comprehend all of God's revelation completely or infallibly. We "see through a glass, darkly" (1 Cor. 13:12 KJV). And we remain sinners, even at our very best. Perhaps one reason God has left this particular matter in doubt, at least among so many faithful Christians, is that by these differences we will be reminded of just how much we truly need one another. The Bible should never be interpreted alone, without the Spirit and the help of others. The Holy Spirit works through us. If all the church is involved in interpreting the Bible, as it should be, then no faithful Christian, or single part of the visible church, should be seen as unfaithful simply because he or she holds a view of baptism that differs from mine or that of my tradition.

THE DEFINITION

"Baptism" derives from the Greek word *baptisma* and denotes the action of washing or plunging in water (Acts 2:41). From the earliest days of Christianity baptism has been a rite of initiation. By this watery sign, made in the triune name of God, people are openly admitted into the life and community of the church. All agree that baptism is the symbolic door into the church.

Though some disagree, most Christians believe that baptism is primarily God's act, God's sign, God's pledge, because it is God who promises his presence in it. Furthermore, baptism functioned in the Bible and in the early church as a gracious mark of Christian identity. By it one took on a new name, a new life, and a new identity. Your Christian baptism, at least according to the earliest records we have of this rite, mattered a great deal.

The historical origins of Christian baptism are primarily traced to OT ritual purifications. Ancient pagans had ceremonial washings, but no one seriously doubts that Christian baptism had its roots in the baptism of John the Baptizer. Why John adopted this rite is not clear, but Jesus himself gives his authority to the act by submitting to it himself (Matt. 3:13) and by commanding that all his followers submit to it as part of their obedience to him (Matt. 28:19).[2]

The simple historical facts are relatively clear at this point. Christians have always been baptized as a sign of their allegiance to Jesus Christ, and from the very beginning they have baptized new converts to the Christian faith. Attempts to replace water baptism have been made through various means. Some have made these attempts in hopes of avoiding some of the problems associated with the act of baptism itself. For example, a baptism of fire or the Holy Spirit, according to Matthew 3:11, has been historically offered, now and then, as a replacement for water baptism. But the profound reality of the Christian symbol remains. A few may try to avoid this, but most instinctively know better. Though the meaning and mode of baptism remain controversial, the simple fact is that the reality itself remains profoundly important.

This underscores another important point often missed by modern believers, namely, the relationship between symbol and ritual. Early Christians, living in a premodern context, had little problem understanding how symbol and reality were intimately connected. They would never have spoken the way many of us do when we refer to baptism as a "mere" symbol. For them symbols and rituals, when authorized by Jesus and practiced by his devout followers because of his commands, were effective and power-laden signs. The emphasis of the early church was never opposed to ritual so much as it was committed to helping people understand (via discipleship) the various Christian rituals (which were simple and few) in their proper context. By catechism and liturgical practice the earliest Christians sought to continually underscore the importance of symbol for obedience to Jesus.[3]

Theologian Laurie Guy has helpfully suggested that Christian baptism was ultimately rooted in the Jewish understanding of the human person as a whole. The Jews did not separate what was done to the body from what was done to the soul: "Baptism was thus inextricably intertwined with faith, as the body side of believing. It was a symbolic action paralleling prophetic actions such as that of Isaiah's going naked (Isa. 20:2–3) or Jeremiah's wearing a yoke (Jer. 27:2–7) in order to portray the future."[4] Baptism was, in this understanding, a kind of acted parable. Augustine argued that baptism set in motion what it symbolized, thus making it a crucial rite, though one which clearly recognized that faith and repentance were "coessential."[5]

THE DESIGN

Baptism in water clearly was universal in the early Christian church. It was accepted and practiced always and everywhere as the self-evident beginning and foundation of the Christian life. By it people were admitted into the visible church. In its form it was a simple action. A person went into or under the water in the name of Jesus (Acts 19:5) and/or the name of the Trinity (Matt. 28:19). Geoffrey W. Bromiley, an Anglican, has correctly noted that "immersion was fairly certainly the original practice and continued in general use up to the Middle Ages."[6] The type of water and the circumstances of administration, he adds, "are not important, though it seems necessary that there should be a preaching and confession of Christ as integral parts of the administration (cf. Acts 8:37)."[7]

The earliest Christian believers seemed to have experienced very little strife regarding baptism, despite the fact that there was a wide variety of practices that evolved over the course of the first few hundred years of the church. I must add, though, that scholars do not all read the early church evidence the same way. What we do have is a consensus, at least regarding the first few hundred years, which suggests there was a great deal of flexibility in actual baptismal practice. In the record of the early church there is evidence for infant baptism, child baptism, adult baptism (including those born into Christian families), immediate baptism (upon profession of faith), delayed baptism (sometimes for as long as several years), and even various modes of baptism (though the *Didache*, a second-century guide, points to immersion as the mode to be used). Baptist scholar Kevin Roy helpfully concludes, "All that can be said with certainty is that within the one catholic church there was both development and variety in baptismal practices until at least AD 400."[8] Interestingly, when there was contention in the early church the debates were more likely about issues that do not concern us today; among them were questions such as, "Was a baptism performed by heretics legitimate?" or, "Was there forgiveness for sins committed after baptism?"

As you will discover in the views presented in this book, the question of the design of baptism is clearly one of the central issues in the modern debate. Who should be baptized? And how should baptism be administered? These are some of the questions that divide the four contributors. Two contributors believe that infants should be baptized, and two do not. Two believe "immersion only" constitutes baptism, while two do not. And all four have a different explanation for what actually happens in baptism. It is helpful to note that, in spite of these differences, there is a good bit of common ground among all four writers. Adult baptisms are still conducted within the churches represented by all four contributors. And all four consider confession of faith in Jesus Christ, as well as gospel repentance, to be important, indeed essential.

Furthermore, there are many biblical associations with water baptism that would be commonly noted by all four contributors. Take Titus 3:5 and its reference to "washing" as a simple example. None of the contributors believe baptism saves a person on the basis of water operating on the person by some kind of magic. The cleansing water of biblical imagery is linked with the blood of Christ on one side of the biblical parallelism, while on the other side we can see the purifying work of the Holy Spirit (1 John 5:6, 8) in reconciling sinners to God. Baptism displays these redemptive actions by sign. Bromiley sheds light on how we can agree while still holding to very real differences when he says that "baptismal grace is brought into proper relationship to the work of God" when we gain a better understanding of the rite and our common agreements. He concludes that "we [should] remember that behind the external action there lies the true baptism, which is that of the shed blood of Christ."[9] Whatever constitutes baptismal grace, the divine action, whether real in some sense or only symbolic, is ultimately rooted in the substitutionary work of Jesus Christ alone.

After thinking about this subject for five decades I have come to understand what I now believe to be a crucial point missed in most contemporary Christian discussions about baptism. We conveniently and often unconsciously make a separation between "form" and "essence." The views presented in this book all come from Western Christian theologians. The difference this makes can be seen by looking at the debate from beyond our better known Western discussions. The late Alexander Schmemann, an Eastern Orthodox liturgical theologian, argued correctly that "the proper understanding of this sacrament is not merely an intellectual but ... an existential necessity." By this he meant that any consideration of baptism must move beyond debate about forms and methods, which are based on intellectual points or rational interpretations of the Christian mystery. The reason for this observation is actually quite simple—baptism in the NT and in early Christian understanding seems to bring us into a reality that transcends such categories. Schmemann makes this observation:

> In the early Church the terms "likeness" and "pattern" most obviously refer to the "form" of Baptism, i.e., to the immersion of the catechumen in water and his rising up from it. Yet it is this very form which manifests, communicates, and fulfills the "essence," is its very "epiphany," so that the term "likeness," being the description of the form, is at the same time the revelation of the "essence." Baptism being performed "in the likeness" and "after the pattern" of death and resurrection therefore is death and resurrection. And the early Church, before she explains—if she explains them at all—the "why," the "what," and the "how" of this baptismal death and resurrection, simply knew that to follow Christ one must, at first, die and rise again with Him and in Him; that Christian life truly begins with an event in which, as in all genuine events, the very distinction between "form" and "essence" is but an irrelevant abstraction. In Baptism—because it is an event—the form and the essence, the "doing" and the "happening," the sign and its meaning coincide, for the purpose of one is precisely to be the other, both to reveal and to fulfill it. Baptism is what it represents because what it represents—death and resurrection—is true. It is the representation not of an "idea" but of the very content and reality of the Christian faith itself: to believe in Christ is to "be dead and have one's life hid with Him in God" (Col. 3:3). Such is the central, overwhelming, and all-embracing experience of the early Church, an experience so self-evident, so direct, that at first she did not even "explain" it but saw it rather as the source and the condition of all explanations, all theologies.[10]

But one does not need to understand the "essence" of baptism to receive the reality. To make our various differences regarding form and manner an end in themselves is to create an impoverished context in which to worship the living God. And it makes grace an abstract reality, or so it seems to me. It finally misses the important point of baptism and the Lord's Supper by making these sacred symbols something less than a joyful sharing of our life with Christ in mystical union. It does this by reducing them both to a mere obligation to be performed or fulfilled.

Some evangelical Protestants are not as likely to see that sacrament (God's action or gift) and symbol must be held together because there is a vital relationship between them. Baptist theologian G. R. Beasley-Murray notes this well: "Where the objective gift is emphasized, there is always a danger of falling into the misinterpretation of an automatic result. Where the symbolic nature is stressed, the tendency is to look upon baptism as a superfluous addition which supplies nothing important. A complete view of baptism will hold together symbol and sacrament, and dissolve neither into the other."[11]

It seems evident to me that the essential biblical point made in texts like Galatians 3:26–29; Colossians 2:12; and Romans 6:1–11 is this: Baptism brings us into union with Christ. The phrase Paul consistently employs in such texts is "in Christ." The sequence of thought employed here, argues Beasley-Murray, "permits no other interpretation" at the end of the day. And the tenses used leads one to understand the central idea here: "All of you who were baptized into Christ have clothed yourselves with Christ" (Gal. 3:27). Beasley-Murray concludes, "The two actions were coincident in time. With this basic conception, union with Christ in his death and resurrection is closely related."[12]

THE DIVISION

In spite of these clear biblical texts and the consensus in the early church, the debates and divisions over baptism have continued since the fourth and fifth Christian centuries, especially since the East and West divided in AD 1054 through the "Great Schism." Baptismal debates and the resultant separation in church communions have proliferated in the West, especially through the divisions that followed the Protestant Reformation of the sixteenth century.

The deep tragedy of this division was perhaps never as

apparent as on a cold January day in 1527 when Felix Manz, a Swiss Protestant minister who had rejected the practice of infant baptism, was put to death by drowning in the River Limmat. Manz had openly confessed his simple faith by writing, "We bring together those who are willing to accept Christ, obey the Word, and follow in his footsteps. We unite them by baptism, and leave the rest to their present conviction." Ulrich Zwingli, the Protestant Reformer, said of men like Felix Manz, "Let him who talks about going under [the water] go under." In this incredible act one evangelical Protestant killed another evangelical Protestant for the crime of seeking to obey God with a clear conscience.

This event prompted the authors of a marvelous book on the nature of this sad division over baptism to ask the $64,000 historical question, "How could so strange a thing happen just ten years after the beginning of the Reformation in Europe?" These two ministers, coming from different positions on the practice of baptism, conclude that "[this] happened because the Reformation of the sixteenth century rediscovered the New Testament gospel, but failed to re-create the New Testament church."[13] Perhaps they are correct. But if this was true in the sixteenth century, what about today? Thankfully, we no longer kill one another over differences about baptism, but we seem to have a deep aversion to the role doctrine played in the thought of the Protestant Reformers. Recovering the essence of the NT church will be no easy task today, especially in an age committed to easy solutions and pragmatic results.

The authors quoted above further observed that the Reformers rediscovered the gospel and preached it with great effect on multitudes, to the conversion of many. In doing so they transformed both church and culture by tearing down the framework of medieval Christendom. "But when they were required to replace that framework and to cater to those converts," write Bridge and Phypers, "they faltered and became confused and divided. The division of Protestantism into Lutheran, Calvinistic and Anglican forms shows this. The later subdivision of Calvinism into Presbyterian, Independent and Baptist denominations underlines it further."[14]

Another problem clinging to modern Protestants is that baptism is commonly seen only as the baptism of individual persons who understand what they do in very individualistic ways. Even where infant baptism is practiced the problem remains, since parents often have no place for the church community in the nurture of their baptized children. The idea that the primary emphasis in baptism is on incorporation into Christ's death and resurrection—thus baptism being seen as initiation into the one church (Eph. 4:3–6)—is practically denied because of two common caricatures. The first caricature sees baptism as nothing more than a personal insurance policy that the one baptized will go to heaven; the second reduces baptism to receiving a name or to getting into the membership of a particular church within a certain cultural expression. These caricatures plainly "promote an individualistic baptismal concept."[15] They also fail to address the issue of how the church and baptism actually relate to one another. As a pastor I often faced this problem when people wanted baptism for themselves or their children but no relationship to a particular church at all. The contributors to this book all seek to keep this vital connection in mind and thus contribute positively to the healing of certain aspects of our sad disunity.

THE DREAM

Is it possible that a study like this one, where the reader is brought squarely into the middle of one of the greatest controversies that still divides Christians, could help us attain a deeper experience of unity? I actually believe it can. This is one of several reasons why I accepted the offer to serve as this book's general editor and to work with these four writers.

The contributors are all deeply devoted to the Christ revealed in Holy Scripture. They believe that salvation is found only in Jesus Christ. You can only be saved in and through his life, his death, his burial, and his resurrection. They also believe that those who would be disciples of Jesus must repent of their sins and have faith in the Son of God. They further agree that Scripture should function as the canon (rule) of all faith and practice. This belief is what theologians have commonly called "the norming norm," and it simply means that Scripture judges tradition, including that of each writer in this book. Theologian James D. G. Dunn gets this right when he concludes, "For a faith that centers so much on the incarnation it can hardly be otherwise, since that faith invests paramount and normative significance in the revelation of a specific life and ministry in a particular time and pale in history, and our only witness/access to that life and ministry is through the New Testament."[16]

Finally, the recovery of the power of symbol and the attendant importance of visual images in the modern world suggest to me that the importance of baptism might be recovered even while we disagree about its exact meaning. How can this be done? By a careful reevaluation of the biblical, cultural, and historical factors that have shaped each of us in drawing our particular conclusions about Christian baptism.

Increasingly dark clouds of secularism and postmodernism impact both church and culture in the West. This context provides a new opportunity for the church to deal with issues that have commonly divided us—baptism, for example. British Baptist theologian Richard Kidd concludes, "The world is already too racked with pain and conflict to permit Christians the luxury of adding to its fragmentation by internal arguments about baptism." He then writes:

> I can no longer work ... with a stark and uncompromising contrast between believers' baptism, which is right, and infant baptism, which is wrong. Rather, I am discovering here two histories of the one sign we call baptism, both of which are proper responses to social and cultural encounters across the years.... These histories simply cannot be mixed, nor should one be allowed to replace the other; for in both these ways, the proper integrity of each would be destroyed.... But I would like to think I can participate in and celebrate the integrity of what is other, without threat to what is profoundly my own.[17]

The message of Christian baptism speaks powerfully to the developing "spirituality" of modern culture. While multitudes are seeking meaning and purpose in life through a myriad of ways, Christians can keep saying to a confused world, "Jesus is Lord." And baptism keeps such a confession central to our Christian faith and community. By working to understand our differences, we can demonstrate to the world that we love one another. We may still disagree, and perhaps we should for the present time, but we've come a long way since the time of the

Reformation. When we consider what Zwingli did to poor Felix Manz, we can safely say that not all the changes that have ensued over the years are for the worse. Perhaps a book like this can foster renewed discussion among thoughtful Christians, all the while encouraging them to study the Scriptures more carefully and thus to love Jesus Christ more deeply.

Introduction: Division, Differences, and a Dream

1. See Donald Bridge and David Phypers, *The Water That Divides: A Survey of the Doctrine of Baptism* (Fearn: Christian Focus Publications, 1998).

2. Laurie Guy (*Introducing Early Christianity: A Topical Survey of Its Life, Beliefs, and Practices* [Downers Grove, Ill.: InterVarsity, 2004], 217–18) notes that Christian baptism likely had its roots in the Jewish practice of baptizing proselytes. "It would be odd," he writes, "if Christians began an initiatory or proselyte baptism and the Jews subsequently took on a similar practice at a time of animosity with Christians. Therefore an arguable case can still be made for Christian baptism having links with already-existing Jewish proselyte baptism."

3. See Bernard Cooke and Gary Macy, *Christian Symbol and Ritual* (New York: Oxford Univ. Press, 2005). This book wonderfully supports the point made in this particular paragraph.

4. Guy, *Introducing Early Christianity*, 219.

5. Cited in Guy, *Introducing Early Christianity*, 219 n. 8.

6. Geoffrey W. Bromiley, "Baptism," in *Evangelical Dictionary of Theology*, ed. Walter A. Elwell (Grand Rapids: Baker, 1984), 113.

7. Ibid.

8. Kevin Roy, *Baptism, Reconciliation and Unity* (Carlisle: Paternoster, 1997), 4.

9. Bromiley, "Baptism," 114.

10. Alexander Schmemann, *Of Water and the Spirit: A Liturgical Study of Baptism* (Crestwood, N.Y.: St. Vladimir's Seminary Press, 1974), 55–56.

11. G. R. Beasley-Murray, *Baptism Today and Tomorrow* (London: Macmillan, 1966), 23–24.

12. Ibid., 28.

13. Bridge and Phypers, *Water That Divides*, 75.

14. Ibid., 76.

15. Eugene L. Brand, "The Rites of Initiation as Signs of Unity," in *Baptism and the Unity of the Church*, ed. Michael Root and Risto Saarinen (Grand Rapids: Eerdmans, 1998), 131.

16. James D. G. Dunn, "Baptism and the Unity of the Church in the New Testament," in *Baptism and the Unity of the Church*, 78.

17. Cited in Bridge and Phypers, *Water That Divides*, 179.

Chapter One

BAPTIST VIEW

Baptism as a Symbol of Christ's Saving Work

BAPTIST VIEW

Baptism as a Symbol
of Christ's Saving Work

Thomas J. Nettles

IT'S A MATTER OF DEFINITION

Recently I received an unusual note from a theology student. "I was completing an assignment in systematic theology," he wrote, "and came to the conviction that I had not been saved. In the process of reading through the material, I cried out to God for forgiveness, and he saved me." This person is a church member preparing for ministry. When he comes to me for advice, what shall I tell him? That he is not yet saved because he is not yet baptized? Does he need to go before the church, professing his faith in Christ through believer baptism? My answer to him has everything to do with the theology of baptism.

Here is a definition that I think reflects the biblical standard for this ordinance: *Baptism is the immersion in water of a believer in Jesus Christ performed once as the initiation of such a believer into a community of believers, the church.* This baptism signifies the believer's confidence that Christ's work was complete for his forgiveness and justification and indicates his desire for unity with the church, Christ's community of the new covenant, purchased at the price of his blood. No saving efficacy inheres in either the form or the matter itself. The person baptized has no scriptural warrant to believe that in baptism Christ's saving activity is initiated, augmented, or completed. In its symbolism, however, it sets forth the saving gospel of Christ both in its objective and subjective aspects. It pictures the historical event in the life of Christ that brought to fruition the purpose of his incarnation, namely, to give his life as a ransom for many. It pictures the believer's conscientious testimony that Christ's acceptable sacrifice alone allows a sinner to approach God in the confidence of being accepted. It pictures the present experience of the believer in his awareness that when he was dead in trespasses and sins, God "made [him] alive with Christ" (Eph. 2:5) by the powerful operations of the Holy Spirit. The power that is necessary to produce this change is "like the working of his mighty strength, which he exerted in Christ when he raised him from the dead and seated him at his right hand in the heavenly realms, far above all rule and authority, power and dominion, and every title that can be given" (Eph. 1:19–21).

BAPTISM IS IMMERSION

That the word translated "baptize" (Greek *baptizō*) literally means "immerse" is a matter of little, if any, dispute. *Strong's Exhaustive Concordance* gives the meaning as "to make whelmed, i.e., fully wet" or "to cover wholly with a fluid."[1] A standard Greek lexicon defines *baptizō* and its cognates as "dip, immerse,... plunge, sink, drench, overwhelm."[2] In his study of the word, George Beasley-Murray gives the meaning of *baptizō* as "dip, immerse, submerge" and observes, "Despite assertions to the contrary, it seems that *baptizō*, both in Jewish and Christian contexts, normally meant 'immerse,' and that even when it became a technical term for baptism, the thought of immersion remains."[3]

John Chrysostom, Martin Luther, and John Calvin all argue that the word means "immerse." Luther states, "I would have those who are to be baptized completely immersed in the water, as the word says and as the mystery indicates.... This is doubtless the way in which it was instituted by Christ."[4] Calvin writes, "The word 'baptize' means to immerse, and it is clear that the rite of immersion was observed in the ancient church," but "the details [of mode] are of no importance."[5] The irony of this concession is that it comes in a section in which Calvin vehemently criticized many of the unauthorized forms that intruded into the practice of baptism in the Roman Catholic Church. "Let us learn," he admonishes, "that there is nothing holier or better or safer than to be content with the authority of Christ alone."[6] So we should all agree. And thus immersion should be the practice of all.

BIBLICAL SURVEY: JOHN'S BAPTISM

The first mention of baptism in the NT occurs in the description of the ministry of John the Baptist in Matthew 3:6. Those who repented of their sins and were willing to receive instruction concerning how to live as a manifestation of repentance were baptized (Matt. 3:6–8; Luke 3:9–14). This involved a "knowledge of salvation through the forgiveness of their sins, because of the tender mercy of our God" (Luke 1:77–78). John's ministry represented a departure from the flesh/national principle ("we have Abraham for our father") of recognizing the people of God (Matt. 3:9–10). He announced a new principle that would mark off God's people, namely, the purifying work of the Spirit (Matt. 3:10–12). Trees that did not bear fruit would be cut down, and the chaff would be burned. Only those who bore fruit could be considered the true children of Abraham.

The apostles noted John's ministry as the beginning of a new way of defining the people of God. The qualifications for selecting an apostle to replace Judas included one who had been with them "beginning from John's baptism to the time when Jesus was taken up from us" (Acts 1:22). When Peter preached at the house of Cornelius, he began, "I now realize how true it is that God does not show favoritism but accepts men from every nation who fear him and do what is right"; he went on to relate how God had enforced this idea through the ministry of Jesus, "beginning in Galilee after the baptism that John preached" (Acts 10:34–37). John's baptism as an inauguration of the new covenant led naturally to more complete knowledge of the way of salvation.

THE BAPTISM OF JESUS

Jesus himself submitted to John's baptism to identify himself as a proponent of his message and as a fulfillment of righteousness. His approval of John carried important value for the ministry of Jesus. Not only did he establish a connection with the prophetic material (cf. Mal. 3:1), he put himself in position to begin a gradual and persistent pedagogical task of refining the understanding of his messianic role, the nature of salvation, and the identification of the people of God. He used John's identification of him as the Lamb of God as a means of demonstrating the hypocrisy and deceitfulness of the Pharisees (Luke 20:4–5).

Beyond that he tells us something important about baptism itself. His baptism indicated for himself, like others, an entire consent of mind and heart to the truth of John's message that Jesus was "the Lamb of God, who takes away the sin of the world (John 1:29) and that repentance marks the covenant people of God (cf. Luke 13:3, 5; 15:7, 10). In addition, he announced that only by death, burial, and resurrection would the promised salvation be effected. Retroactively he gave fullness of meaning to his baptism when he said, "I have a baptism to undergo, and how distressed I am until it is completed" (Luke 12:50). The case is similar in Mark 10:38: "Can you ... be baptized with the baptism I am baptized with?" Moreover, he united by public demonstration with others who also believed this message announced by John. He marked off baptism as that ordinance in which the recipient gives a visible testimony to a cordial persuasion that Jesus alone in his unique person and work qualifies as Savior.

Baptism did not confer any status on Jesus that he did not already possess or create any conviction that he did not already have. Unlike us, he did not receive baptism as testimony to personal salvation, but as confirmation of his personal commitment to effect it for others through his future baptism of suffering and resurrection to glory. Those who follow him in baptism do so in the same confidence of Jesus' unique qualifications and work.

BAPTISM IN THE BOOK OF ACTS

The baptisms in the book of Acts confirm this pattern. Genuine repentance involved knowledgeable dependence on Jesus Christ in his death, burial, and resurrection as the only hope of forgiveness of sins.

Peter as a Baptizer

When Peter finished his sermon on the day of Pentecost, many in the crowd "were cut to the heart" and asked, "What shall we do?" (Acts 2:37). Peter responded, "Repent and be baptized, every one of you, in the name of Jesus Christ for the forgiveness of your sins. And you will receive the gift of the Holy Spirit" (2:38). Four elements define this event: the message preached, the response of repentance and faith, the receiving of baptism, and the mention of those who received baptism. The message consisted of a demonstration that Jesus was Messiah, whose death by crucifixion issued in his exaltation so that he now bestows redemption, forgiveness of sins, salvation, and the Holy Spirit. The required response, manifest genuinely by "all whom the Lord our God will call," was repentance and baptism particularly in the name of Jesus Christ. Those who were baptized were the ones "who accepted his message" (2:41).

In this instance, it is clear that only those capable of personal response were baptized. No baptisms are recorded for any except those who received—heard, understood, and responded positively to—the message that Peter preached. As in the case of John the Baptist in his ministry, this first occurrence of a post-resurrection baptism was given only to those who personally recognized the justice of God in the message and embraced its truth (cf. Luke 7:29–30).

As in the case of John, the baptism signified all that is involved in repentance for the forgiveness of sins. The baptism "in the name of Jesus Christ" (Acts 2:38) identified their present acceptance of the truth preached about Jesus—a message that this group in particular had rejected so vigorously that they had nailed him to a cross (2:23, 36). A genuine repentance and a true belief must now be seen precisely in terms of a reversal of their verdict about that one name—Jesus—who was being proclaimed as the Christ (2:36). Only three years before, many had rejected the message and thus the baptism of John the Baptist; in so doing, they denied the Lamb of God whom John announced. Jesus, moreover, had confirmed his own message and purpose in line with that baptism. The message of John was now matured and fully consummated in the preaching of the apostles (cf. Luke 7:24–28; 20:1–8). Receiving baptism, the ordained symbol of confessing John's kingdom message, clearly indicated repentance from sin and unbelief as well as heartfelt, death-defying belief in the message and meaning of Jesus as Messiah. Only such believers were baptized; those who would not be baptized had surely not believed.

Philip, Baptism, and the Kingdom of God

Philip's work in Samaria assumed that believing the message about the kingdom of God and the name of Jesus Christ preceded baptism: "When they believed Philip as he preached the good news of the kingdom of God and the name of Jesus Christ, they were baptized, both men and women" (Acts 8:12). Their being baptized constituted the means of their identification with others who believed this same message. The "good news of the kingdom of God" had been preached from the beginning of the ministry of John the Baptist, was continued by Jesus, and now we find Philip following suit.

The kingdom of God as preached by John, Jesus, and the apostles is the visible manifestation of the glory, wisdom, and sovereign power of God through the person and work of Christ for the salvation of sinners. Although the kingdom involves a display of God's omnipotence, it goes beyond the reign of God through mere omnipotence. His kingdom will demonstrate not only his reign of justice by condemnation but of redemption by an inscrutably wise mercy (cf. 2 Thess. 1:5–12; 2:13–14). This could only be done by means of the mystery of the Messiah's humiliation in the incarnation for the free salvation and sanctification of rebels.[7]

This kingdom consists of a fellowship of the reconciled, redeemed, forgiven, justified, and sanctified out of every people group on earth. They have submitted to Christ in his humiliation, for they have seen in this scheme, by God's efficacious call, both the power of God and the wisdom of God. Their public confession that Jesus is Lord and their acknowledgment of faith in his work of justification are made in baptism. For this reason, when the Samaritans believed the preaching of the good news about the kingdom of God, their status as subjects of the kingdom was marked with baptism (Acts 8:12). The external display of the Spirit's operations came later through apostolic prayer.

The eunuch from Ethiopia heard the gospel in the context of the prophecy in Isaiah 53 (cf. Acts 10:26–39). Taking verses 7 and 8 as his starting point, Philip "told him the good news about Jesus." As a culmination of the continuing stream of prophecy about the Messiah, he must have included Jesus' baptism at the hands of John and its implications for those who believed, as well as Jesus' command to make disciples and baptize them.

With great enthusiasm, the eunuch asked Philip to baptize him. After doing so, Philip was taken away by the Holy Spirit.

PAUL AND BAPTISM

Acts 9 records the conversion and baptism of Saul. After brief words from Ananias, the text states succinctly, "[Saul] got up and was baptized" (v. 18). Paul's account in Acts 22 gives more detail of the event. The specific appointment of Paul as a special witness is mentioned: "The God of our fathers has chosen you to know his will and to see the Righteous One and to hear words from his mouth. You will be his witness to all men of what you have seen and heard" (22:14–15). Then the command for baptism comes: "Get up, be baptized and wash your sins away, calling on his name" (v. 16).

Does this mean that in baptism Paul was to consider his sins as being washed away? The text does not support this viewpoint. His baptism identifies him with the Jesus whom he recently persecuted and whose mission was defined in terms of his submission to the baptism of John. The washing away of sins is connected with calling on Jesus' name. The participle should be considered instrumental: "by calling on his name." This phrase duplicates Peter's use of the same verse in Joel in the sermon at Pentecost (Acts 2:21). Paul uses it in Romans 10:13: "Everyone who calls on the name of the Lord will be saved." There he shows that such calling is the mouth's expression of the heart's conviction that salvation depends on the atoning work of Christ verified as acceptable by the resurrection. At his conversion, therefore, Paul expressed his persuasion that Jesus was Lord and Christ and that the resurrection represented the culmination of Christ's atoning work. In his heart—in the seat of his moral judgment and affections—he knew that Christ's death was necessary for salvation. The resurrection meant that the propitiation was accepted, and now, by the power of an incorruptible life, the Righteous One lives and intercedes for us before the Father (cf. Rom. 4:24–25). His baptism was a public witness to his cordial union with Christ in the entire redemptive transaction.

Because of this strong image present in baptism, Paul used it as a teaching tool in pressing the implications of salvation on the churches. When some inferred falsely that since increased sin meant superabounding grace (cf. Rom. 5:20–21) we should continue in sin, Paul reminded them of what they had confessed in their baptism: "Don't you know that all of us who were baptized into Christ Jesus were baptized into his death? We were therefore buried with him through baptism into death in order that, just as Christ was raised from the dead through the glory of the Father, we too may live a new life" (Rom. 6:3–4). Your confession in baptism, Paul insists, contradicts the false logic of continuing in sin.

Paul declares that when we are baptized into Christ Jesus, we undergo a vivid reenactment of our participation with Christ in his historical death on the cross. Faith implies that we have come to a verdict of condemnation concerning ourselves and a repulsion concerning our sin. We see our only hope for forgiveness and right standing in Christ's work. Each movement in the baptismal event bears witness to the historically objectified spiritual status that a sinner receives experientially by faith. The picture of being surrounded by the water and emerging from it calls to mind the irreversible purpose assured in Christ's being delivered up to death for our sins and being raised again for our justification, to save us not only from sin's penalty but from its power.

Paul employs this same use of baptism in Galatians 3:27: "All of you who were baptized into Christ have clothed yourselves with Christ." He had emphasized that their justification and adoption came by faith: "So we, too, have put our faith in Christ Jesus that we may be justified by faith in Christ and not by observing the law, because by observing the law no one will be justified.... You are all sons of God through faith in Christ Jesus" (2:16; 3:26). Paul raged against a heresy that sought to add something of religious ceremony (circumcision) to the completed work of Christ in order to complete salvation (cf. 3:1–5; 5:1–6). He insisted that from the cross of Christ flow all the blessings of eternal life and life in the Spirit (cf. 2:20; 3:13–14; 5:11; 6:14–15). Hearing and believing the message of the cross unleashes all the blessings stored in it.

How strange would it be that Paul introduces a new ceremony by which Christ's saving work becomes effectual? Could he really be saying, "Reject the heretical formula of hearing plus believing plus circumcision; instead replace it with hearing plus believing plus baptism"? That interpretation of baptism would run counter to Paul's purpose in Galatians. Their baptism gave a physical presentation of the spiritual certainties involved in faith. Faith is not empty but engages us with the resurrected Christ in his present status of living to make intercession for us. He gained that status through his being a "merciful and faithful high priest in service to God, and that he might make atonement for the sins of the people" (Heb. 2:17). Thus when by faith we are clothed with Christ, baptism illustrates the transaction that actually has taken place. As a divinely ordained manner of expressing an existing confidence, baptism is spoken of as the thing itself. When Paul refers to the Galatians' baptism as being "clothed ... with Christ," he encourages them to remember that Christ's death alone, and no human ritual, bears to them spiritual life.

Paul, Baptism, and the Church at Corinth

This understanding of Paul's distinction between faith and baptism becomes more clearly established in his first letter to the Corinthians. One division in that church focused on baptism (cf. 1 Cor. 1:10–17). So insistent was he that this divisiveness over baptism was a tempest in a teapot that he reminded them, "Christ did not send me to baptize, but to preach the gospel—not with words of human wisdom, lest the cross of Christ be emptied of its power" (v. 17). At the same time, though Christ did not send him to baptize, he could remind them that "in Christ Jesus I became your father through the gospel" (4:15). He became their father in their response through faith to the gospel he preached. They were begotten not by baptism but by the preached word. Luke states the order: "Many of the Corinthians who heard him believed and were baptized" (Acts 18:8).

This experience in Corinth accords with the order expressed in Jesus' missionary commission to his apostles: "Go and make disciples of all nations, baptizing them in the name of the Father and of the Son and of the Holy Spirit, and teaching them to obey everything I have commanded you" (Matt. 28:19–20). The participles take the force of the command to make disciples: go, make disciples, baptize, teach. The order is informative as it previews the obedient work of the apostles in Acts. First they made disciples; next they baptized; then they taught and provided a means for the perpetuity of instruction in the churches thus established. Jesus' command gives an explicit order that his disciples have no right to alter.

Paul, Baptism, and the Obedience of Faith

As he establishes the nature of his ministry at the end of his letter to the Romans, Paul makes it quite clear that baptism and faith are not to be identified:

> Now to him who is able to establish you by my gospel and the proclamation of Jesus Christ, according to the revelation of the mystery hidden for long ages past, but now revealed and made known through the prophetic writings by the command of the eternal God, so that all nations might believe and obey him — to the only wise God be glory forever through Jesus Christ! Amen.
>
> *Romans 16:25–27*

If Paul were not sent to baptize, but nevertheless those to whom he preached were established by his gospel and if his preaching of the "revelation of the mystery" subdued nations to the "obedience of faith" (Rom. 1:5 NASB), he cannot have seen faith as incomplete without baptism. He certainly does not minimize baptism in its proper place as an expression of the relationship established by faith, but he views it as separate from faith and adding nothing to that which can be gained by faith only.

The phrase "obedience of faith" means the conformity of one's heart to the plain teaching of the gospel: "To the man who does not work but trusts God who justifies the wicked, his faith is credited as righteousness" (Rom. 4:5). Our entire race is bound up in the disobedience of one man to God's law, and rescue from condemnation comes only through the obedience of one, namely, Jesus Christ (cf. 5:19). Seeking favor before God in any way other than through faith in Christ alone and his complete obedience indicates a lack of conformity in heart and mind to the gospel. Paul's goal was to speak the gospel with such clarity and boldness that the nations would cease striving after a righteousness of their own and submit entirely to the way of faith. This is the "obedience of faith."

Paul, Baptism, and the Philippian Church

In Philippi Paul found Lydia at a place of prayer (cf. Acts 16:13–14). When he spoke the gospel to her, "the Lord opened her heart to respond to Paul's message" (v. 14). Then she and her household were baptized (v. 15). Also in Philippi, a jailer, saved from self-inflicted death by Paul's intervention, asked, "What must I do to be saved?" (v. 30). Paul's answer, "Believe in the Lord Jesus, and you will be saved—you and your household" (v. 31), provoked the jailer to take him to his house and have his entire household instructed in the gospel. They washed the wounds of Paul and Silas, and then they were baptized (v. 33). Paul and Silas joined the jailer and his family for a meal, "and [the jailer] was filled with joy because he had come to believe in God—he and his whole family" (v. 34). The order is consistent: instruction, belief, baptism.

PETER AT THE HOUSE OF CORNELIUS

We go now to visit Peter at the house of Cornelius. Before visitors invited Peter to make the trip, God had given him a lesson that broke the back of the ceremonial laws about uncleanness (cf. Acts 10:1–18). Recounting this vision, Peter began his sermon with his realization of the expansiveness of God's purpose in the gospel to include all nations (vv. 34–35). He then preached about the saving work of Jesus. When he reached the point of application—"All the prophets testify about him that everyone who believes in him receives forgiveness of sins through his name" (v. 43)—the Holy Spirit fell on the Gentiles with irrefutable evidence. The circumcised believers were astonished that the Spirit had been poured out even on Gentiles. On the basis of this evidence, Peter ordered and arranged for their baptism.

When Peter reported this to the church in Jerusalem some of the circumcised believers criticized him for entering the house of the uncircumcised (Acts 11:2–3). Peter recounted the lesson that God had taught him through the vision of unclean things—a lesson objectified in the conversion of the Gentiles. This reminded Peter that the baptism of John, which had called for repentance as the mark of divine grace, also prefigured the baptism of the Holy Spirit through which the body of Christ is formed and fitted for service (v. 16; cf. 1 Cor. 12:12–13). When the evidence demonstrated that the Spirit had surely come upon them, Peter acknowledged that baptism in water was warranted.

PETER'S TEACHING ABOUT BAPTISM

Did Peter believe that baptism saved? The book of Acts shows that he placed great importance on baptism in its connection with preaching and the consequent expressions of repentance and faith. Was the connection between baptism and faith vital and effectual in sealing salvation to the penitent sinner?

In his first letter Peter says, in effect, that baptism saves:

> This water [the flood] symbolizes baptism that now saves you also—not the removal of dirt from the body but the pledge of a good conscience toward God. It saves you [these words are supplied by translators] by the resurrection of Jesus Christ, who has gone into heaven and is at God's right hand—with angels, authorities and powers in submission to him.   *1 Peter 3:21–22*

In answering the question posed by this passage, we must see three ways in which the Bible speaks of things that save. The first group of Scriptures speaks of God's immediate work in salvation. He begins it in eternity, establishes it in time, works it into personal experience, maintains its power and purpose in the saints until death, and infallibly brings it to consummation (cf. 1 Pet. 1:3–5). These aspects of salvation reside solely in the purpose, intrinsic virtue, and personal unfrustratable power of the triune God. They do not change from generation to generation but are consistent with our creation in his image. Only these things may be said to save us in a direct sense:

> In his great mercy he has given us new birth into a living hope through the resurrection of Jesus Christ from the dead.   *1 Peter 1:3*

> Since we have now been justified by his blood, how much more shall we be saved from God's wrath through him!   *Romans 5:9*

The second group speaks of means that operate in various ways congruent with the rational and moral nature of salvation. The mind and heart must consent to truth divinely revealed.

Faith seizes upon the object in whom righteousness is immutably established. Confession naturally flows from the heart of the regenerated person and gives evidence that the root of salvation power is present (cf. Rom. 10:10). Though no person can save another in an absolute sense, the one who carries the word of truth establishes the context in which sinners are saved: "Whoever turns a sinner from the error of his way will save him from death and cover over a multitude of sins" (Jas. 5:20). Sinners are urged to save themselves: "Save yourselves from this corrupt generation" (Acts 2:40). Paul told Timothy that in his faithful stewardship of the ministry he would save both himself and his hearers (cf. 2 Tim. 4:16).

A third group uses salvation language in reference to the symbols of his passion that Jesus commanded his church to observe. This involves concrete pictures — fit symbols — to express and call to mind the divine mercy in salvation.

In his institution of the Lord's Supper, Jesus said, "Drink from it, all of you. This is my blood of the covenant, which is poured out for many for the forgiveness of sins" (Matt. 26:27–28). Through metaphor, Jesus calls the wine "my blood of the covenant" and asserts that forgiveness of sin directly depends on its being poured out. When we eat the bread and drink the wine, we call to mind that he alone is the true bread and his blood is true drink, and it is only by them that we have eternal life. Metaphorically, the cup and the bread procure eternal life.

It is within the sphere of this third group of Bible passages that we understand Peter's statement that "this water symbolizes baptism that now saves you also." We must see the statement in the context of Peter's full argument.

Making the Application to Peter's Argument

The major point of the context is clear and simple: Christians should endure persecution patiently because in the end their triumph is secure through Christ (1 Pet. 3:13–22). A secondary idea in the text, but primary in the larger theology of the passage, also is clear: Jesus Christ has suffered, not for his own sins but for the sins of others for the purpose of bringing them to God. This suffering directly produces salvation.

We must bear this in mind when we look at the waters of the flood that saved the "few people, eight in all" and the antitype of "baptism that now saves [us]." Judgment and wrath for one is salvation for another. The flood killed all other inhabitants but bore up Noah and his family away from all those who were condemned to die. The death of Christ, his baptism of wrath, brought judgment on him and showed its certainty for all who remain in sin, but bears up and away from condemnation those for whose sins he died.

The text says that baptism does not remove the moral filth natural to life in this body. It affirms rather that we know that God has dropped his charges of condemnation against us because of Christ. Baptism represents the confident reliance on the judgment that Christ took for us, which judgment becomes our salvation. Baptism itself does not remove the damnable filth but expresses one's confidence that only the propitiatory death of Christ saves. We also express assurance that only the resurrection of Christ seals this transaction. His death satisfied all the demands of God's law so that, as Peter preached at Pentecost, death had no legitimate claim on its victim. The resurrection warrants the pledge, the affirmation after inquiry, of a good conscience unto God.

As a clear symbol of the saving reality, baptism stands as a perpetual witness to the historical substance of salvation and because of that connection is said to save us.

CIRCUMCISION AND BAPTISM

Another substantial issue concerning the biblical teaching on baptism concerns its relationship to OT circumcision. I will make three observations. First, according to Colossians 2:11–13, circumcision and baptism have a positive relationship but not a direct analogy. Circumcision typifies not baptism but regeneration, that is, a "putting off of the sinful nature." Paul reiterates this in Galatians: "Neither circumcision nor uncircumcision means anything; what counts is a new creation" (Gal. 6:15). Baptism includes a picture of fulfilled circumcision and much more. Baptism sharpens the focus, not only on the inner life of the sinner but on Christ's historical work by which life, forgiveness, and righteousness come. It depicts both the quickening work of the Spirit in raising sinners from death to spiritual life and the complete salvation purchased by the death, burial, and resurrection of Christ.

A second issue concerns discontinuity and continuity. Circumcision signified three aspects of God's purpose. It marked off the messianic nation in the flesh from the Gentiles, pointed back to the righteousness imputed to Abraham by faith (Rom. 4:11–25), and pointed forward to the true circumcision of heart that would mark off the true spiritual children of Abraham (Rom. 2:25–29).

Paul's refutation of the Judaizers assumes the fulfillment of these three things: "For it is we who are the circumcision, we who worship by the Spirit of God, who glory in Christ Jesus, and who put no confidence in the flesh" (Phil. 3:3). This signifies the new birth, the completed work of Christ, and justification by faith alone apart from works of righteousness.

The third point in recognizing the analogy between baptism and circumcision argues that we must affirm and not deny the explicit characteristics of the new covenant. As stated in Jeremiah 31:31–34, and recalled in Hebrews 8:8–12, the partakers of this covenant have the law already in their minds and hearts. Also, those in the new covenant do not need to be taught, "Know the Lord," for they already know him. They have been taught of God in regeneration. They already are seen as justified, because God has forgiven their wickedness and removed the guilt of their sins. The positive qualifications manifest in this announcement of God's covenant admit the application of its sign only to those who are qualified.

CONCLUSION

In summary, here are a few of the conclusions drawn from my study and reflection on baptism:

- Beginning with the preaching of John the Baptist, the mark that signified one's entrance into the kingdom of God was submission to baptism. This mark indicated a heart-change manifest in repentance, which, according to the new covenant, would be the distinguishing characteristic of its subjects. Jesus and the apostles continued to practice baptism with this signification.
- First-order symbolism of baptism is the death, burial, and resurrection of Christ. Receiving baptism gives testimony that one accepts the position of Jesus as Son of

God and as Lamb of God and recognizes his sacrifice as the only means by which sin may be forgiven.

• Second-order symbolism expresses the spiritual position of the one baptized. It depicts the act of faith by which one unites with Christ in his atoning work and confesses that the death Christ died was in the person's place. It embraces the resurrection as the power that motivates and energizes a new life of mortification of sin. The person being baptized acknowledges the necessity of repentance as a kingdom trait.

• The only ones who receive baptism are those who hear the gospel and believe. We can point to no person who, when he or she received baptism, was not fully instructed in the gospel material concerning the life, death, and resurrection of Christ. They trusted in Christ, not baptism. Those who come into a Baptist church having been baptized as an infant, therefore, would have to give a credible profession of a work of grace and give testimony to it through believer baptism. By the same token, those seeking to enter a Baptist church from churches that see baptism as a constituent element of justification would not be received without believer baptism.

• Regeneration fulfills the ritual of circumcision. Circumcision had no intrinsic efficacy but pointed forward to the new creature and the new covenant. Even so, baptism points beyond itself to the effectual reality of Christ's saving work and the Spirit's application of this work to the elect. Just as circumcision had nothing to do with the justification of Abraham (Rom. 4:10–11), so baptism has nothing to do with the justification of the believing sinner.

• Baptism was not optional. Its significance as a testimony to salvation in Jesus' name, and the command issued by the Lord himself, made it the natural and most precisely expressive concomitant to saving faith. One cannot be received, therefore, into church membership without this kind of baptism.

• Baptism is a church ordinance and is normally performed by those whom the church has set aside for the instruction and discipline of the church, namely its pastors. On occasion the church may give authority to others to baptize if special reasons warrant or compel such a circumstance.

Postscript: By the way, the theology student whose note I mentioned at the beginning of this chapter made a profession of faith in a local Baptist church and, in obedience to the scriptural presentation of baptism, was immersed before the congregation as his pledge and the church's pledge of a cleansed conscience before God.

A REFORMED RESPONSE

Richard L. Pratt Jr.

Tom Nettles has presented the doctrine of baptism held by most Christians who call themselves Baptist. He presents no surprising exceptions to the norm and offers a substantial defense of the position. His view has similarities to outlooks on baptism that characterize the Reformed tradition, but a number of important differences stand out as well. In my response, I will comment on his three main points: (1) baptism must be performed by immersion; (2) baptism only symbolically represents saving grace; and (3) baptism is only for those who profess faith.

BAPTISM AS IMMERSION

In the first place, Nettles argues that baptism in the NT means immersion. On a positive note, most Reformed theologians would agree that the word *baptizō* and related terms had connotations of dipping or immersing in the first century. As Nettles points out, however, Beasley-Murray's extensive study of the word concludes that it "normally meant 'immerse.'" This qualification of "normally" is significant in that it indicates a flexibility that may actually extend the meaning of the term beyond what we often mean by literal or complete immersion. In fact, scholars continue to debate the precise meaning of baptism because the evidence is not entirely clear.

We also agree that archaeological and biblical evidences strongly suggest that Christian baptism was most likely performed by some kind of immersion. It may not have entailed the complete submerging of candidates, as Baptists are inclined to believe, but biblical examples seem to indicate that a significant quantity of water was required for the rite.

Despite these agreements, however, the Reformed tradition disagrees that the Scriptures dictate the amount of water and the degree to which a candidate should become wet. In matters like these, Reformed theology distinguishes between the circumstances and elements of worship. Believers are free to use prudence in the former but must carefully follow the dictates of Scripture in the latter. In the case of baptism, the performance of the rite in the name of the Trinity and with water is certainly an element of worship, but it is the Reformed position that the Scriptures do not clearly direct many of the circumstances related to baptism.

Appeals to biblical examples may be helpful but not conclusive. For example, to my knowledge there is no indisputable example in the NT of baptism being performed in a corporate worship service, as it is so often done today. Yet this does not mean that baptism must not be performed in corporate worship. On the contrary, the Scriptures do not give such details because they grant flexibility. In much the same way, the amount of water with which a person must come in contact and the precise manner in which water is applied are matters of circumstance in which prudence must rule. One would question the wisdom, for instance, of requiring an Eskimo convert to build a warm bath or to wait for summer before receiving baptism by total immersion.

To argue by analogy, it is common for Baptists to exercise freedom in many circumstances as they observe the Lord's Supper. The elements are served in individual cups and wafers, even though this was not the NT pattern. In fact, Paul spoke of "the cup" and "the one loaf" (1 Cor. 10:16–17) and drew specific theological implications for the unity of the body of Christ in the oneness of the loaf. Even so, few Baptists insist on observing these details because the Scriptures do not clearly insist on them. Observing the Supper is an element of worship, but the precise manner in which we serve Communion is a matter of circumstance.

This complexity is why John Calvin and others allow for freedom in aspects of the performance of baptism that are not explicitly taught in Scripture. Liberty of conscience requires that we not insist on matters that go beyond what the Scriptures teach.

BAPTISM AS SYMBOL

Nettles's second major assertion is that baptism merely symbolizes divine saving grace. I would agree wholeheartedly that "baptism and faith are not to be identified" (p. 34). In this respect, Reformed theology concurs with him. Salvation is by grace through faith and not inextricably tied to the rite of baptism. Yet I disagree strongly when he asserts that "the person baptized has *no scriptural warrant* to believe that in baptism Christ's saving activity is initiated, augmented, or completed" (p. 25, emphasis mine). Such a statement is at best a hyperbole. Nettles himself discusses a number of passages precisely because they at least *seem to indicate* that there is some scriptural warrant for connecting baptism and salvation.

Nettles argues for a symbolic view of baptism in large measure because he sees it as the way to safeguard other central teachings of the Scriptures. He holds NT doctrines such as *sola fide* and *sola gratia* very firmly. Sinners are justified by faith alone and saved by divine grace alone. It is important to safeguard these doctrines, but we must be careful to do so in biblical ways. Nettles concludes from these sure biblical doctrines that this baptism can only be symbolic, as if this were the only logical way of keeping salvation by grace through faith intact. But viewing baptism as nothing more than a symbol is not the only way to relate these essential Protestant doctrines to the rite. As the chapters in this book illustrate, many Protestant traditions have understood the relationship quite differently without compromising salvation by grace through faith. Reformed theology, for example, characterizes the relationship between baptism and saving grace as a mystery in an attempt to do justice both to these central doctrines and to the close connection that the NT establishes between baptism and divine grace.

In my estimation, the weakest portion of Nettles's argument for the symbolic character of baptism is his designations of three levels of salvation language in the NT. In the first place, he speaks of aspects of the work of God for salvation that "do not change from generation to generation but are consistent with our creation in his image. Only these things may be said to save us in a direct sense" (p. 36). Nettles admits that God "establishes [these aspects of salvation] in time" (p. 36). Yet one still wonders if this definition is adequate. Why should we believe that the

Scriptures speak in a direct sense about salvation only when they address permanent, unchanging aspects of salvation? This is particularly problematic because the death and resurrection of Christ were historical events that took place at a particular time, but surely the biblical claims about these events speak of salvation directly.

His second category of salvation language speaks of the "means of salvation." Faith, the word of God, and the like fall into this category nicely. Yet he does not include baptism in this category, unlike other Christian traditions that do. He does not explain why baptism does not fall into this category; he only asserts it.

His third category is defined as "the symbols ... that Jesus commanded his church to observe" (p. 37). He urges that this is the meaning of "baptism ... now saves you" in 1 Peter 3:21. In this passage Peter draws an analogy between baptism and the waters of Noah's flood, and I wonder if Nettles's second category is not more appropriate. Floodwaters were the means by which Noah and his family were saved, not a mere symbolic act. It would appear that Nettles's desire to put baptism into this third category obscures the connection that Peter made.

Put simply, while I would agree that there are many ways in which Scripture uses salvation language, Nettles does little more than assert three categories that correspond to his theological assessments. His distinctions are by no means convincing.

BAPTISM FOR BELIEVERS

Nettles's third assertion is that baptism is only for those who are believers. His discussion focuses primarily on the relation of circumcision and baptism. He is correct when he argues that we must be cognizant of discontinuities between the OT and NT, but he offers little justification for the kinds of discontinuities he draws between circumcision and baptism. In his view, circumcision in the OT is seen as a foreshadowing of regeneration in the NT rather than as a foreshadowing of NT baptism. This outlook is unfortunate because it misses one of the clearest conceptual parallels between OT and NT faith. As I argue in my chapter, clear symmetry exists between the OT and NT in this regard. In the OT, physical circumcision pointed to the need for inward spiritual circumcision; in the NT, physical washing in baptism points to the need for inward spiritual washing. The parallels are between two outward acts and the inward realities they represent.

In my estimation, Nettles's distinction between the old and new covenants offers one of the most problematic aspects of his chapter. On the basis of Jeremiah 31:31–34, he argues that all people in the new covenant are true believers. In other words, while some unbelievers were included in covenant with God in the OT, they are not in the NT. Sadly, his discussion fails to reckon with the reality that NT writers constantly addressed. Jesus did inaugurate the new covenant in his first coming, but he did not bring any of the new-covenant promises in Jeremiah 31:31–34 to their complete fulfillment in his first advent. The new-covenant community will consist exclusively of truly regenerate people only when Christ returns, which is why Hebrews 10:26–31 warns that God will still judge "his people" (v. 30) and that apostasy is possible for one who "has treated as an unholy thing the blood of the covenant that sanctified him" (v. 29). When the current impurity of the new-covenant community is acknowledged, it opens the way for understanding why children of believers may receive baptism in the NT as the sons of believers received circumcision in the OT. Outward circumcision of adults and sons pointed to the need for inward circumcision for adults and sons; outward cleansing in baptism points to the need for inward cleansing for both adults and children as well.

In summary, I am grateful for Dr. Nettles's clear presentation of the Baptist position. While I believe his views have much merit, I remain unconvinced that his position presents the most comprehensive posture to be taken on this subject.

A LUTHERAN RESPONSE

Robert Kolb

The guiding principles of biblical interpretation that shape Professor Nettles's investigation of baptism—his three ways salvation language is used—provide a helpful vantage point for assessing differences between a Baptist and a Lutheran understanding of baptism. In regard to his third type of salvation language, we agree that God's messengers in the Bible do indeed use symbols of the passion, particularly (but not only) in OT prophetic foreshadowings of the Messiah's coming, to announce God's saving action for sinners. In addition, it is important to realize that probably about the same percentage of the biblical writers' language should be interpreted literally, as is the case with the language of most Americans today—a good percentage but certainly not everything we say or write. In regard to his second type of salvation language, I believe, as he does, that God establishes his saving relationship with sinners by giving them the gift of trust in him through language that presents what God has done for us in Christ in a clear and understandable manner. That every part of God's saving activity is always rational seems doubtful, for the mystery of our salvation is great and beyond our comprehension, even as is his gracious decision to create us as human creatures in the first place, but we do agree that it comes in propositional form. The moral dimension of our salvation comes as a result and not as a cause of God's action, for God does truly turn us from our sins in order that we may enjoy human life as he designed it in the first place. This life is certainly a life that obeys his commands and carries out his will in the world.

Nettles's description of the first kind of salvation language forms for Lutherans the vital framework for the other two kinds of salvation language. He notes that God indeed begins salvation in eternity, through his unconditioned choice of those whom he decided to make his own (cf. Eph. 1:3–14)—a salvation God has established in time, working it into personal experience and maintaining its power and purpose in the saints until death as he infallibly brings this salvation to consummation. Where Nettles and I seem to differ is on the means by which God establishes the saving relationship between himself and his people and how he works it into our personal experience and maintains its power and purpose in our lives.

When two people engage in an exchange of ideas, as important as what each says is what each does not say that the other does say and what emphasis they put on specific issues. Readers of this book will notice in our chapters that not only the concepts of the Word of God and sacrament but also of sin and human reactions to the Word are approached quite differently. At the level of our presuppositions, we each presume certain things about God's way of acting, about his use of human language, and about the state of fallen human creatures entrapped in their sinfulness. Nettles and I have been reading the same texts from Scripture, but he can conclude that "the person baptized has no scriptural warrant to believe that in baptism Christ's saving activity is initiated, augmented, or completed" (p. 25). My reading of the NT draws me to the opposite conclusion. This can be explained, as Nettles states at the beginning of his chapter, as "a matter of definition" or presupposition and perhaps also as a matter of direction (p. 25).

The fundamental difference between us, from my perspective, is the definition of how God works to save sinners. Since I believe that God's creative word brought all of reality into existence and that his word continues to govern and preserve all of God's creation, I believe that this word, when it appropriates the human language of the gospel of Jesus Christ as its instrument, is performative speech. It is God's re-creative tool for changing the reality of the lives of sinners through the forgiveness of sins. Therefore, an approach that only finds a picture or symbol in baptism seems to miss the point that biblical writers take for granted: God is at home in his creation, and he selects elements from the material created order, like human language, as well as human flesh and blood, to carry out his saving will.

Finding baptism to be no more than a "teaching tool" (p. 31) seems to me to deny that God is at work, effecting his will to save, not just picturing it, when he comes at us with his word in all its forms—oral, written, and sacramental. Relegating forms of his word to the role of only pointing to heavenly realities seems to me to reflect the ancient Greek philosopher Plato's definition of a great gap between spiritual or heavenly reality and the material created order. It does not conform to the biblical image of the way God the Creator works. To advance our common understanding of baptism, Nettles and I need to engage in an examination of our presuppositions about God's use of human language. Until we can sort out whether God's word in point of fact actualizes and realizes his will as it comes to sinners, or whether the words of his people can do no more than point the attention of sinners to the heavenly realities of God's disposition toward them through Christ, we will be doomed to talk past each other. For on the basis of this definition rest the ways in which we view the passages that talk about God's action of turning sinners from their sin and turning them to God in trust.

In the light of that discussion, we could proceed to talk about the amount of water needed to carry out God's command. Baptism consists of the word of God joined with water. The water is placed within the setting of God's command. He commands to baptize in order to make disciples (a process that also involves maturing after baptismal new birth through further use of the word in oral and written forms as fellow believers teach one another, according to Jesus in Matt. 28). Because the chief element is the word of God, the amount of water needed to constitute the sacrament has never seemed as critical as the proper understanding and use of the word for Lutherans.

It is clear that the widespread usage of the Greek word *baptizō* indicated immersion, and early Lutherans did immerse infants, according to pictorial accounts. But by the time of Jesus, the word *baptizō* was used for applying cleansing water to tables, and the Pharisee probably did not expect that Jesus would have immersed himself when he was "surprised" that Jesus had not (literally, according to the Greek text) "baptized himself" before the meal (Luke 11:38).[1] Nevertheless, however preferable immersion may be to other forms of applying the water, what is vital for this act of God is his word.

Nettles's opening account raises the fundamental question for Lutherans about the direction in which the action of baptism is moving. Lutherans believe that God wants to give his people assurance based on more than their own efforts or feelings. Therefore, they contend that the primary "move" in baptism is from God to us, and only when he has spoken to us are we able to converse with him. Only when he has made us his new creation through actually burying our sinful identity in Christ's tomb and raising us to new life with him are we able to walk in the footsteps of Jesus (cf. Rom. 6:3–11; Col. 2:11–15). The student who came to decide that he was not saved, on the basis of the surface of his account, now had only his crying out to God for forgiveness as the foundation and source of his consolation in the gospel. Our memories of our coming to God with a cry for forgiveness help sustain us on the good day, but when temptations to doubt come, we need the assurance that stands in the promise of God quite distinct from our own feelings and memories. I suspect that behind this story Nettles would also insist that God is the guarantor of salvation and that God had come to that student through some form of his word.

He points out that "the powerful operations of the Holy Spirit" (p. 26) is what makes us alive with Christ, according to the apostle in Ephesians 2. It is obvious that the essayist does not believe that the Holy Spirit operates with his power through an automatic ritualistic or magical bestowal of that power, nor through a New Age-style bubbling up of some sort of spirit from our own depths. In Titus 3 Paul employs language somewhat similar to Ephesians 2 to describe the human dilemma apart from Christ and the "kindness and love of God our Savior." He saved us "not because of righteous things we had done, but because of his mercy," and he did so "through the washing of rebirth and renewal by the Holy Spirit, whom he poured out on us generously through Jesus Christ our Savior" (Titus 3:4–5). The consolation of bruised reeds and smoldering wicks (Isa. 42:3) takes place on the basis of the external, independent word of the Lord that can pierce through doubt and despair and uncertainty in the darkest hours of flickering faith. For the sake of all believers in such moments, our conversation about God's ways and means of working with us must continue.

A CHRISTIAN CHURCHES/ CHURCHES OF CHRIST RESPONSE

John D. Castelein

Christians in the Christian Churches/Churches of Christ will find much in Dr. Nettles's chapter to agree with: (1) the Scriptures are the primary source to resolve theological disagreements rather than denominational creeds (helpful as they may be at times); (2) all first-century Christian baptism was by immersion; (3) Christ's church should not change this original mode of baptism; (4) God's covenant with his new people in the NT replaces the "flesh" principles of the OT with Spirit-life principles; and (5) infants are not proper candidates for baptism as they cannot hear the word, believe the word, and repent while calling on Jesus as their new Lord.

Nettles proposes this biblical standard for baptism: "Baptism is the immersion in water of a believer in Jesus Christ performed once as the initiation of such a believer into a community of believers, the church" (p. 25). One important truth needs to be added: the church (both in its universal essence and local expressions) is the body of Christ. The Scriptures do not warrant separating incorporation into Christ by faith from a later incorporation into a local church by baptism.

On the one hand, it is true that "no saving efficacy inheres in either the form or the matter [of baptism] itself" (p. 25). We believe that the water in and of itself (*ex opere operato*—which means it is effective just by virtue of performing the ceremony) does not channel grace independently of the word being heard, believed, and received by the individual in genuine repentance.

On the other hand, there *is* saving efficacy, by God's grace, in actions that actualize the obedience of the faith. Faith in Paul's theology includes the mind believing facts, the heart trusting promises, and the will obeying commands of the Lord. It may be correct to say we are saved through "faith only" in the sense that one understands this faith to be the complete human response and not just mental assent.

The epistle of James defines faith differently. James clearly teaches that "faith alone" (used only once in the Bible in Jas. 2:24) is dead and useless unless it is actualized in obedience. When it comes to the role of immersion as obeying the Lord's command, the apostle James's words about Abraham come to mind: "his faith and his actions were working together [when he was in the process of sacrificing Isaac], and his faith was made complete by what he did" (Jas. 2:22). It is absolutely true, as Nettles states, that in baptism Christ's saving activity is not "initiated, augmented, or completed" (p. 25), but James certainly teaches that faith itself is completed in obedience.

Baptism expresses "the believer's confidence" (p. 25) in Christ's past and completed work on the cross precisely because it so dramatically actualizes, in the here and now, faith's repentance (dying to the world) and faith's profession of Jesus as new Lord. The analogy with marriage is helpful. One does not go through the marriage ceremony because one has already been wed through one's prior genuine love for the spouse but precisely because one wants to enter before witnesses into a covenantal relationship.[1]

Nettles's treatment of Acts 22:16 raises important questions. Why attach the washing away of sins directly with "calling on his name" (the participle) but not with "be immersed [i.e., baptized]" (the verb of command)?[2] There is one subtle but important reference to calling on the Lord's name that he does not cite (he mentions Acts 2:21 and Rom. 10:10–13). It is found in Acts 2:38, where the Greek speaks of being baptized "upon" (*epi* in Greek) the name of Jesus. Peter's command to those who cry out because they believe his message is that they must repent and be baptized while calling on the name of the Lord. There should be no divorcing of professing Jesus with one's mouth, embracing him as Lord in one's heart, and surrendering one's body to him in immersion (expressive of one's burial to the world and beginning of new life).

Nettles's treatment of Romans 6:3–4 raises even more questions.[3] There are several places (especially in the gospel of John) where believers are said to believe "in" Jesus and the preposition is *eis* in Greek ("unto," "into"). In this passage in Romans (cf. Gal. 3:27; see Matt. 28:18), the act of immersing parallels the act of believing in that it also is "into" Jesus Christ and "into" his death (both times *eis* is used). There is no need to reject either of these affirmations, because faith and baptism work together.

Nettles insists that Paul's argument against the serious undermining of grace because of the conduct of disobedient believers (cf. Rom. 6:1) merely uses their baptisms as a symbolic picture (p. 32).[4] However, this undervalues the actual role of baptism as the occasion of dying to the condition of being "in Adam" and coming to life "in Christ" (cf. Rom. 5). It is crucial to Paul that the sinner in Adam who is wed to God's implacable law die to the law "through the body of Christ" in order to wed the Risen Lord (Rom. 7:1–4).

We do not need to deny that baptism unites us with Jesus Christ by incorporating us into his death and resurrected life unless we have artificially divorced faith from immersion and then claim that the uniting with Jesus has already occurred at the instant of faith. As I observe in my essay, conversion involves several components working together (hearing, believing, repenting, obeying in being immersed, and professing Jesus as Lord). We believe we are commissioned to preach and practice the kind of conversion found in the NT that keeps these elements united as much as possible. Neither one's baptism nor one's repentance makes Christ's saving work "effectual," but both are means by which we accept his work as a personal gift of grace.[5]

That the Spirit was at work in Jesus' conception and that Jesus from birth was the incarnate Son of God all true believers affirm. However, that in Jesus' baptism nothing was added or that baptism did not change Jesus' status (p. 28) is questionable. If nothing more, at least in his own baptism Jesus was anointed by the Spirit as the Christ, the Messiah. For those who in faith and repentance embrace God's offer of grace on the cross, it seems fair to say that at baptism the forgiveness of sins and the gift of the indwelling Spirit are added (Acts 2:38) and that the pollution of sins is subtracted (Acts 22:16).

Christian Churches/Churches of Christ will find Nettles's repeated emphasis on John the Baptist's ministry and his claim that John brings about the "inauguration of the new covenant" (p. 27) strange, to say the least. John faithfully prepared the way of the Lord, and Jesus greatly valued his ministry by continuing his call for repentance and immersion; yet, while he valued John's ministry as bringing the kingdom nearer, Jesus revealed, in fact, that the least person in the kingdom was greater than John was (cf. Matt. 11:11–12).

When the disciples asked the risen Lord about when this promised kingdom of God would come (Acts 1:6), Jesus urged them to wait for events soon to be happening (Pentecost). Just as his own baptism inaugurated Jesus' ministry, so the Spirit's descent at Pentecost would launch his second body, the church, to complete his mission on earth. It is, therefore, startling to read that those who responded on the day of Pentecost to Peter's call for repentance and baptism were, in fact, receiving "the ordained symbol of confessing John's kingdom message" (p. 29). Apollos knew all about John's baptism but was still in need of being taught about baptism in Jesus' name (Acts 18:26).

Chapter 1: Baptist View (Thomas J. Nettles)

1. *Strong's Exhaustive Concordance of the Bible: Compact Edition* (Repr., Grand Rapids: Baker, 1997), 18 (in "Greek Dictionary of the New Testament" section).

2. W. Bauer, W. F. Arndt, and F. W. Gingrich, eds., *A Greek-English Lexicon of the New Testament and Other Early Christian Literature* (Chicago: Univ. of Chicago Press, 1957), 131.

3. George Beasley-Murray, "*Baptizō*," in *New International Dictionary of the New Testament*, ed. Colin Brown (Grand Rapids: Zondervan, 1975), 1:144.

4. Martin Luther, *Three Treatises: The Babylonian Captivity of the Church* (Philadelphia: Fortress, 1960), 191.

5. John T. McNeill, ed., *Calvin: Institutes of the Christian Religion* (Philadelphia: Westminster, 1960), 2:1320.

6. Ibid., 1319.

7. For the biblical display of both aspects of the kingdom—humility and mercy—before power and judgment, see 2 Thessalonians 1:5–12; 2:13–14; Titus 2:11–14.

Chapter 1: A Lutheran Response (Robert Kolb)

1. See Albrecht Oepke, "*Baptō*," in *Theological Dictionary of the New Testament*, ed. Gerhard Kittel and G. W. Bromiley (Grand Rapids: Eerdmans, 1964), 1:530.

Chapter 1: A Christian Churches/Churches of Christ Response (John D. Castelein)

1. For a detailed comparison of baptism with the wedding ceremony, see F. LaGard Smith, *Baptism: The Believer's Wedding Ceremony* (Cincinnati, Ohio: Standard, 1989).

2. A similar theological prejudice separates forgiveness of sins and the gift of the Spirit from the command to be immersed (baptized) in Acts 2:38–39 and attaches it only to the command to repent. That "repent" is plural and "be baptized" is singular in no way eliminates immersion from the promised gifts. "Repent" may well be addressed to physical Israel as a nation and "be baptized" to every penitent believer with a body to be surrendered.

3. For thorough examinations of all the scriptural references to immersion in the NT, the following books are highly recommended: G. R. Beasley-Murray, *Baptism in the New Testament* (Grand Rapids: Eerdmans, 1962); Jack Cottrell, *Baptism: A Biblical Study* (Joplin, Mo.: College Press, 1989); Rees Bryant, *Baptism: Why Wait? Faith's Response in Conversion* (Joplin, Mo.: College Press, 1999).

4. In essence, Nettles claims in his essay that whatever the NT says of baptism is always intended merely as a symbol of faith or as a metonymy for faith. Theology professor Jack Cottrell of Cincinnati Christian University has traced this significant reduction of baptism's role in conversion to the theological revolution brought about by Swiss Reformer Ulrich Zwingli. See his "Baptism According to the Reformed Tradition," in *Baptism and the Remission of Sins: An Historical Perspective*, ed. David Fletcher (Joplin, Mo.: College Press, 1990), 39–81.

5. When Paul in 1 Corinthians 1:17 states that Christ did not send him to baptize, it is clear from the context that Paul is not denying how very important baptism is; rather, he is denying that baptism bonds the candidate to the person performing it, as if one adheres to the name of the baptizer. In fact, baptism is one of three basic realities that should unite all Christians: (1) all are baptized into Jesus' name (not into Paul's name); (2) Christ is not divided; and (3) one and the same Jesus Christ died for all (1 Cor. 1:13).

Chapter Two

REFORMED VIEW

*Baptism as a Sacrament
of the Covenant*

REFORMED VIEW

Baptism as a Sacrament
of the Covenant

Richard L. Pratt Jr.

Most Christians who identify themselves as Reformed or
Calvinists affirm that baptism is a sacrament of the covenant of
grace. Although different branches of the Reformed tradition
highlight different aspects of baptism, the major Reformed confessions and catechisms emphasize that baptism is both sacramental and covenantal.[1] For this reason, I will discuss first the
Reformed concept of baptism as a sacrament, and then I will
focus on baptism's covenantal character.

BAPTISM AS SACRAMENTAL

In its own way, the Reformed understanding of baptism is
highly sacramental. That is, Reformed theology views baptism
as a mysterious encounter with God that takes place through a
rite involving physical elements and special ceremony. Through
this encounter, God graciously distributes blessings to those
who participate by faith and also judgment to those who participate without faith.

The technical use of the term "sacrament" derives from
Ephesians 5:32 in the Vulgate, where *sacramentum* translates the
Greek word *mystērion*, meaning "mystery." Prior to the Reformation, "sacrament" denoted a variety of rites that were thought
to lead to experiences of God's grace in ways that exceeded the
limitations of human understanding. After varying formulations

competed for dominance in the medieval church, the Council of Trent (1545) finally assigned the term "sacrament" to seven central rites: baptism, confirmation, holy Eucharist, penance, extreme unction, orders, and matrimony.[2]

John Calvin and most other Protestant leaders rejected the Roman Catholic sacramental system but retained its vocabulary, applying the term "sacrament" only to ordinances instituted by God himself (cf. Westminster Confession of Faith 27; Belgic Confession 33). They insisted that baptism and the Lord's Supper, and only those two ordinances, were instituted by Christ and confirmed by his apostles as sacraments for the church. They also retained the idea that the sacraments are "means of grace," vehicles through which God is pleased to apply grace to believers (Westminster Confession of Faith 14.1). Reformed theologians insisted, however, that such grace only accompanied the proper administration and appropriation of the sacraments.

This conception of sacraments as "means of grace" provides a helpful framework for examining some of the distinctives of the Reformed doctrine of baptism. In particular, it is useful to examine the Reformed assertion that there are both connections and separations between baptism and divine grace.

Connections between Baptism and Grace

On the one side, calling baptism a "means of grace" distinguishes the Reformed tradition from Protestants who conceive of baptism as a mere symbol. Unlike Baptists and Anabaptists, who tend to speak of baptism only as an "ordinance," Calvinists have characteristically spoken of baptism not only as an ordinance but also as a sacrament or a mystery, a rite through which God applies grace.

Although the Reformed vocabulary of "sacrament" was adopted from Roman Catholicism, the basis for recognizing sacraments as means of grace was inferred from Scripture. With specific regard to baptism, it is worth noting that the NT never describes baptism as something ordinary or natural; it never speaks of baptism as a mere symbol. The language of "sacrament" was sustained by Reformed churches precisely because the NT ties baptism so closely to the bestowal of divine grace.

For example, Paul spoke of baptism as "the washing of rebirth and renewal by the Holy Spirit" (Titus 3:5). He also wrote that, through baptism, believers are united to Christ and die to sin (cf. Rom. 6:3–7). Peter, in turn, when asked what was required for salvation, replied, "Repent and be baptized, every one of you, in the name of Jesus Christ for the forgiveness of your sins" (Acts 2:38). Elsewhere, Peter boldly declared, "Baptism ... now saves you also—not the removal of dirt from the body but the pledge of a good conscience toward God. It saves you by the resurrection of Jesus Christ" (1 Pet. 3:21). These and many other NT passages seem to indicate that baptism is much more than a symbol. In the language of the Bible, spiritual realities such as rebirth, renewal, forgiveness, salvation, and union with Christ are intimately associated with the rite of baptism.

The Westminster Confession of Faith (27.2) acknowledges this biblical evidence in sacramental terms: "There is, in every sacrament, a spiritual relation, or sacramental union, between the sign and the thing signified: whence it comes to pass, that the names and effects of the one are attributed to the other." A "sacramental union" exists between "the sign and the thing signified." A mysterious union, a "spiritual relation," exists between baptism and grace so that "the names and effects" which the Scriptures use to speak of divine grace may also be attributed to the rite of baptism. When the Scriptures attribute "the names and effects" of God's saving mercy to the rite of baptism, they speak in a sort of theological shorthand by metonomy, leaving the precise relationship mysterious or unexplained.

Reformed theology concurs with Scripture that there is more than meets the eye in the rite of baptism. Spiritual realities occur in conjunction with baptism, but the Scriptures do not explain in detail how baptism and divine grace are connected. Thus, Reformed theology speaks of the connection as a "sacramental [i.e., mysterious] union." It is in this sense that Reformed theology rightly calls baptism a "sacrament."

Separation of Baptism from Divine Grace

On the other side, Reformed theology understands the connection between baptism and grace in ways that distinguish it from those who identify divine grace too closely with the rite. In contrast to Roman Catholicism, Orthodoxy, and a variety of Protestant churches that speak of baptismal regeneration or of the necessity of baptism for salvation, Reformed theology separates baptism from the bestowal of divine grace in certain respects.

To understand this dimension of Reformed theology, it helps to see how closely baptism is linked to the preaching of God's Word.[3] John Calvin identified two marks of the true church: the preaching of the Word of God and the proper administration of the sacraments.[4] In many respects, these two marks comprise two ways in which the Word of God comes to his people: the preached Word and the visible Word. Because of this close association, Reformed theology has consistently defined the sacramental significance of baptism in association with the preaching of the Word of God.

In Reformed theology, the preaching of the Word in the power of the Spirit is the primary means by which faith and salvation come to those whom God has chosen. No rite may serve this primary role. As Paul put it, "Faith comes from hearing the message, and the message is heard through the word of Christ" (Rom. 10:17).

The Belgic Confession (article 33) reinforces the truth that the sacraments serve a secondary role in connection with the preaching of the Word: "[God] has added these [the sacraments] to the Word of the gospel to represent better to our external senses both what he enables us to understand by his Word and what he does inwardly in our hearts, confirming in us the salvation he imparts to us." The visible rite of baptism is added to the preaching of the Word in order to confirm what is preached and what we experience through the inward work of the Holy Spirit in connection with preaching. As article 33 also declares, through this external confirmation, God "nourish[es] and sustain[s] our faith."

The answer to Heidelberg Catechism Question 66 echoes this language, explaining that God ordained baptism in order to "make us understand more clearly the promise of the gospel" and to "put his seal on that promise." As the Westminster Confession of Faith (27.1) tells us, the sacraments "represent Christ, and His benefits" and "confirm our interest in Him." It is in this sense that Reformed standards often speak of baptism as a "sign" and "seal" (Belgic Confession 33; Westminster Confession of Faith 27.1; 28.1; Westminster Larger Catechism 162,

165; Westminster Shorter Catechism 92, 94). As a sign, it visibly depicts the truth of the gospel, including among other things the blessings that come to those who exercise saving faith in the preached Word. As a seal, it confirms the truth that saving grace is found only in Christ.

In the Reformed view, baptism does not normally convey spiritual benefits apart from the preaching and reception of the gospel. Rather, it increases our understanding of the preached Word, nourishes and sustains us in our faith, and confirms the benefits that come through saving faith in the preached Word. Reformed theology's emphasis on God's sovereignty and freedom leaves room for the sacraments to work in unexpected ways, but Scripture establishes the norm that the sacraments work in conjunction with the preaching of the Word.

Further, like the preaching of the Word, the sacraments do not guarantee that their recipients will receive the blessings they offer. In this regard, the Westminster Confession of Faith (28.5) reads as follows: "Grace and salvation are not so inseparably annexed unto [baptism], as that no person can be regenerated or saved without it; or, that all that are baptized are undoubtedly regenerated." In this statement are three denials that distinguish the Reformed view from those that too closely identify baptism and salvation: (1) baptism and "grace and salvation" are not utterly inseparable; (2) it is possible for a person to be regenerated or saved without baptism; and (3) not everyone who is baptized is certainly regenerated.

Nevertheless, these denials are followed immediately in this confession (28.6) by an affirmation of the efficacy of baptism, but in terms of divine mystery: "The efficacy of Baptism is not tied to that moment of time wherein it is administered; yet, not withstanding, by the right use of this ordinance, the grace promised is not only offered, but really exhibited, and conferred, by the Holy Spirit, to such ... as that grace belongs unto, according to the counsel of God's own will, in His appointed time."

In the Reformed view, baptism is efficacious; divine grace is "really ... conferred, by the Holy Ghost" through baptism. Even so, the confession declares that this bestowal is mysterious because it is ordered entirely by the freely determined eternal counsel of God. Grace is conferred "according to the counsel of God's own will, in His appointed time." The timing of the bestowal of salvation to those who have received the rite of baptism remains hidden in the mysteries of the divine counsel.

To sum up, Reformed theology holds that baptism is a sacrament and not a mere symbol. At the same time, it distinguishes itself from traditions that too closely associate the rite and divine grace.

BAPTISM AS COVENANTAL

A second major dimension of the doctrine of baptism in the Reformed tradition is its covenantal character. The theology of covenant went through significant developments in the first centuries after the Reformation, but a fuller and enduring version appears in the Westminster standards.[5] In the theology of Westminster, "covenant" denotes the manner in which God condescends to human limitations. The Westminster Confession of Faith (7.1) observes that "the distance between God and the creature is so great, that although reasonable creatures do owe obedience unto him as their Creator, yet they could never have any fruition of him as their blessedness and reward, but by some voluntary condescension on God's part, which he hath been pleased to express by way of covenant." Here "covenant" is a categorical term describing the full breadth of God's revelation of himself to humanity. In this broad sense, there is nothing in the Christian faith that is not covenantal, defined in terms of God's revelation to humanity.

To understand how baptism relates to covenant, we must delve further into Westminster's theology. Divine condescension through covenant takes two basic forms: (1) before the fall into sin, God entered into the "covenant of works" with humanity in Adam (the Westminster Larger Catechism Question 20 refers to this as "a covenant of life"); and (2) he entered into the "covenant of grace" with humanity in Christ. The Westminster Confession of Faith (7.2, 3) declares that "the first covenant made with man was a covenant of works, wherein life was promised to Adam.... Man, by his fall, having made himself incapable of life by that covenant, the Lord was pleased to make a second, commonly called the covenant of grace."

The covenant of works applied to the relationship between God and humanity before sin; the covenant of grace was initiated immediately after the fall into sin, extending from that point in the OT to the end of the NT. Reformed theology has understood the governing principle of both Testaments to be the grace of God in Christ. The Westminster Confession (7.6) declares that "there are not therefore two covenants of grace, differing in substance, but one and the same under various dispensations." OT believers found salvation by placing their faith in the gospel of Christ to come; NT believers find salvation by placing their faith in the gospel of Christ who has come.

When Reformed theology speaks of baptism as covenantal, the sacrament is viewed in the context of the unity of the covenant of grace. The meaning of baptism is not found in the teachings of the NT alone; it is also inferred from the manner in which baptism fulfills OT patterns of faith. This reliance on the covenantal unity of both the OT and NT is stated in general terms when the Westminster Confession identifies the ordinances administered. In the OT, the covenant of grace was "administered by promises, prophecies, sacrifices, circumcision, the paschal lamb, and other types and ordinances delivered to the people of the Jews" (7.5). Yet, "when Christ, the substance, was exhibited, the ordinances in which this covenant is dispensed are the preaching of the Word, and the administration of the sacraments of Baptism and the Lord's Supper" (7.6). Baptism administers the NT dispensation of the covenant of grace in ways that are analogous to the administration of the OT dispensation of that same covenant.

Implications of the Unity of the Covenant of Grace

A number of important aspects of the Reformed doctrine of baptism come to the foreground on the basis of the unity of the covenant of grace. I will discuss four of these: initiation and continuation of life in covenant, external and internal conditions in covenant, visible and invisible communities of the covenant, and believers and their children in covenant.

Initiation and Continuation

The fact that there are two sacraments ordained for the people of God in the NT age draws attention to a set of parallels in the OT. Baptism correlates to circumcision, and the Lord's Supper corresponds to Passover.

It is evident from the Gospels that the Lord's Supper is the fulfillment of the rite of Passover.[6] The Lord's Supper nourishes and sustains believers in their faith by repeated observances much like Passover aided the faithful in the OT. Passover was a lasting ordinance for Israel; it was her way to remember, even to reenact, the deliverance of the nation from slavery in Egypt. In much the same way, the Lord's Supper reenacts Jesus' celebration of Passover with his disciples and reminds us of the significance of his death and resurrection. In this sense, the Lord's Supper focuses on the continuation of life in covenant with God.

Reformed theologians and commentators typically focus on baptism as an initiation into covenant by pointing out a similar analogy between baptism and circumcision. As the Belgic Confession states, "Having abolished circumcision, which was done with blood, he established in its place the sacrament of baptism.... Baptism does ... what circumcision did for the Jewish people" (article 34).

This connection between circumcision and baptism is typically based on Colossians 2:11–12: "In him you were also circumcised, in the putting off of the sinful nature, not with a circumcision done by the hands of men but with the circumcision done by Christ, having been buried with him in baptism and raised with him through your faith in the power of God, who raised him from the dead." NT believers undergo "the circumcision done by Christ" as they are "buried with him in baptism."[7]

The book of Acts reveals that baptism replaced circumcision only through a complex process. The rite of baptism probably has its roots in the washing ceremonies in the temple, as these ceremonies were expanded and applied in various ways in first-century Judaism. Thus the mode of baptism in Reformed theology is largely a matter of indifference.[8] Christian baptism can be associated with the ritual washings that various sects of Judaism observed in their efforts to distinguish themselves as the remnant of Israel. It may also be associated with Jewish proselyte baptism.[9] As Gentiles began to fill the early church, the perpetuation of circumcision among Christians came into question. Jesus apparently never taught on this question, leaving it to his apostles to determine the course of the church. At the council at Jerusalem (Acts 15), the Christian apostles determined that circumcision would no longer be required of NT believers, and that baptism alone would suffice as the initiatory rite for the Christian church.

In the OT, circumcision was the rite of initiation into the covenant of grace. It was established in the days of Abraham as a perpetual ceremony (cf. Gen. 17:12); in fact, to fail to be circumcised was to violate the covenant offered to Israel (cf. 17:14). Reformed theologians draw on this OT pattern and see baptism as an initiatory rite, such that those who receive baptism are initiated into covenant with God. This is why the Westminster Confession (28.1) speaks of baptism as "a sign and seal of the covenant of grace."

Internal and External Conditions

Reformed theology also draws on the analogy between circumcision and baptism to point out that saving faith is required of those who receive baptism. As with circumcision, baptism is not an end in itself. It serves as a visible reminder of the need for God's covenant people to internalize their religion.

In the OT, inclusion in the covenant came about through physical circumcision, but the ideal for ancient Israelites was not that they merely be circumcised in their bodies. To receive eternal covenant blessings they were to be circumcised in their hearts. Moses expressed this ideal as he addressed the people: "What does the LORD your God ask of you but to fear the LORD your God, to walk in all his ways, to love him, to serve the LORD your God with all your heart and with all your soul, and to observe the LORD's commands and decrees .... Circumcise your hearts, therefore, and do not be stiff-necked any longer" (Deut. 10:12–13, 16).

Circumcision of the heart was turning from stiff-necked resistance to the commands of God and committing to faithful living. The prophet Jeremiah used similar language: "Circumcise yourselves to the LORD, circumcise your hearts, you men of Judah and people of Jerusalem, or my wrath will break out and burn like fire because of the evil you have done—burn with no one to quench it" (Jer. 4:4). Physical circumcision expressed externally what was required to be true of the inner person. It called for a deeper commitment to life in the covenant, true repentance, and wholehearted devotion to God and his ways.

In the same way, the NT insists that baptism is not merely an external sign. It not only initiates recipients into a covenant relationship with God but also calls for internalization. Those who receive baptism are to be washed not only outwardly but inwardly as well. As Peter put it, "baptism ... now saves you also — not the removal of dirt from the body but the pledge of a good conscience toward God" (1 Pet. 3:21). Paul confirmed this perspective: "In him you were also circumcised, in the putting off of the sinful nature, not with a circumcision done by the hands of men but with the circumcision done by Christ, having been buried with him in baptism" (Col. 2:11–12).

Visible and Invisible Communities

Since initiation into covenant occurs through outward circumcision and calls those in covenant to inward circumcision, it follows that a division exists in the community of the covenant. Specifically, the covenant community in reality consists of *two* communities: baptized believers and baptized unbelievers.

In Romans 2:28–29 Paul confirmed that there were two groups within the nation of Israel. He spoke of the one who is "a Jew ... outwardly [or visibly]" and one who is "a Jew ... inwardly [or invisibly]," and he concluded that "a man is a Jew if he is one inwardly; and circumcision is circumcision of the heart, by the Spirit, not by the written code." Paul distinguished between the visible and the invisible people of God in the OT. The visible nation of Israel experienced many temporary blessings from God (cf. Rom. 9:4–5), but Abraham's eternal inheritance was granted only to the invisible people of God, namely, those who had the faith of Abraham (cf. Rom. 4:16; Gal. 3:7–9).

The Westminster Larger Catechism (64) extends Paul's distinction between visible and invisible Israel to the NT age by speaking of the invisible and the visible church: the invisible church "consists of the whole number of the elect, that have been, are, or shall be gathered into one under Christ the Head"; the visible church, by contrast, is much larger, including all those who are outwardly a part of the church of Christ, and is "made up of all such as in all ages and places of the world do profess the true religion, and of their children" (62). This is why the Westminster Confession (28.1) speaks of "the solemn admission of the party baptized into the visible Church." Baptism unfailingly initiates people into the visible church, but it provides entry into the invisible church only for those who have saving faith.

Herein lies a vital distinctive of the Reformed doctrine of baptism. The distinction between the visible and invisible church expresses the belief that the visible covenant community of the NT remains a mixture of regenerate and unregenerate people who are baptized. A number of Christian traditions, however, appeal to the promise of the new covenant in Jeremiah 31 to deny this distinction between the visible and invisible church in the NT age. God makes this promise in Jeremiah 31:33b–34:

> "I will put my law in their minds
>   and write it on their hearts.
> I will be their God,
>   and they will be my people.
> No longer will a man teach his neighbor,
>   or a man his brother, saying, 'Know the LORD,'
> because they will all know me,
>   from the least of them to the greatest,"
>   declares the LORD.
> "For I will forgive their wickedness
>   and will remember their sins no more."

This passage indicates that the internalizing of faith and the granting of forgiveness for sin will be true of all who are counted as the people of God in the new covenant, but a vital qualification must be added. Although it is true that we are now in the age of the new covenant (cf. Luke 22:20; 2 Cor. 3:6; Heb. 9:15; 12:24), it is also true that none of the promises of the new covenant have been completely fulfilled.[10] Even members of the new covenant are now threatened with eternal judgment (cf. Heb. 10:26–30). When Christ returns in glory, the visible church will be one and the same with the invisible church. But until that time, the new covenant has only been inaugurated. There are, right now, unbelievers in the visible church. Until the consummation of all things when Christ returns, the distinction between the visible and invisible people of God remains.

Believers and Their Children

A fourth way in which the unity of the covenant of grace informs the Reformed doctrine of baptism is with regard to the candidates for baptism. The Reformed position is that baptism should be applied both to those who profess faith in Jesus Christ and to their children. The Westminster Confession (28.4) declares that "not only those that do actually profess faith in and obedience unto Christ, but also the infants of one, or both, believing parents, are to be baptized. The Belgic Confession reflects the same outlook: "We believe our children ought to be baptized and sealed with the sign of the covenant, as little children were circumcised in Israel on the basis of the same promise made to our children" (article 34).

This covenantal outlook on infant baptism distinguishes Reformed theology from many other traditions. Reformed churches do not baptize children to regenerate them or to remove the curse of original sin. Nor do Reformed churches baptize children simply to indicate the parents' dedication of the child to God. We baptize children to initiate them into covenant with God and to incorporate them into the visible church. As circumcision brought infant boys into the visible nation of Israel, baptism brings children into the visible church.

Reformed commentators readily admit that the NT does not explicitly command or indisputably illustrate the baptism of children. The few references to household baptisms may have included children, but these references are not explicit (cf. Acts 10:44–48; 16:13–15, 30–34).

Why, then, should we baptize children of believers? Reformed theology extends baptism to the children of believers for two main reasons. First, Paul summarized the significance of circumcision for Abraham in this way: "He received the sign of circumcision, a seal of the righteousness that he had by faith while he was still uncircumcised" (Rom. 4:11). For Abraham as an adult, circumcision was a sign and seal of righteousness by faith. If we take this passage as the NIV suggests, circumcision signified and sealed the righteousness that Abraham himself had through faith as an adult. Even so, he was also commanded to circumcise his sons before they even had the opportunity to exercise faith (cf. Gen. 17:12). In much the same way, baptism is rightly applied to adult converts after they profess faith, and rightly applied to their children even though these same children may not be capable of faith.

Second, every stage of the covenant of grace in the OT (Adam, Noah, Abraham, Moses, and David) gave special place to the progeny of believers as the expected—though not guaranteed—heirs of the covenant promises (cf. Gen. 9:9; 15:18; 17:7; Deut. 7:9; Pss. 89:28–29; 132:11–12).

The theology exhibited in this OT pattern explains several significant passages in the NT. For example, Jesus paid special attention to the children of those who followed him, laying his hands on them (Luke 18:15) to confer on them a covenant blessing (Mark 10:16). He also taught with reference to children that "the kingdom of heaven belongs to such as these" (Matt. 19:14), meaning that it belonged to the children who were brought to him and to others like them. It should not be surprising, then, that Peter announced a special place for the children of believers when he said, "The promise is for you and your children and for all who are far off—for all whom the Lord our God will call" (Acts 2:39). The order of priority is the same in the NT as it was in the OT. God's promises are first to believers, second to their children, and third to others who are far off. In a similar way, Paul argued for the sanctification of unbelieving spouses married to believers, noting that "otherwise your children would be unclean, but as it is, they are holy" (1 Cor. 7:14). In Paul's language, being "holy" or "sanctified" was equivalent to being part of the visible church (cf. 1 Cor. 1:2).

In an essay titled "The Polemics of Infant Baptism," B. B. Warfield summed it up as follows: "God established His church in the days of Abraham and put children into it. They must remain there until He puts them out. He has nowhere put them out. They are still then members of His Church and as such entitled to its ordinances."[11] So it is that the Reformed branch of the church baptizes not only adult converts but also the children of believers.

The unity of the Scriptures expressed in the unity of the covenant of grace supplies a number of contours for the doctrine of baptism. Baptism initiates into the covenant, calls for internalization of the faith, distinguishes two communities among those who are baptized, and justifies the baptism of the children of believers. It is in these ways that Reformed theology speaks of baptism as covenantal.

The Reformed tradition shares many viewpoints on baptism in common with other branches of the church. There is "one Lord, one faith, one baptism" (Eph. 4:5). Yet, Reformed theology distinguishes itself from others as it formulates the manner in which baptism is sacramental and covenantal.

PRACTICAL ISSUES:
A FEW QUESTIONS AND ANSWERS

Q: *Should people be rebaptized upon profession of faith?*

A: Reformed churches have strongly opposed rebaptizing anyone who has been baptized in the name of the Trinity. Questions are raised when anomalies occur (e.g., if a person discovers that his or her parents were neither believing nor baptized). Such cases are handled with attention to the particular circumstances and desires of the person in question.

Q: *Should the baptism of infants be required?*

A: In the past, Reformed churches typically insisted that parents in membership have their children baptized. In recent decades, a number of Reformed denominations have encouraged all parents to present their children for baptism but only required that ordained officers of the church have their children baptized.

Q: *Who is qualified to perform baptisms?*

A: Although extraordinary circumstances may call for a baptism to be performed by someone who is not ordained, Reformed churches have urged that only ordained ministers of the gospel perform baptisms under normal circumstances. This practice is usually supported by the apostle's call that "everything should be done in a fitting and orderly way" (1 Cor. 14:40). It is the responsibility of the minister to ensure that baptism is performed in accordance with Scripture.

A BAPTIST RESPONSE

Thomas J. Nettles

I appreciate the clarity with which Dr. Pratt presents the Reformed view of sacramental baptism. As one would expect, his discussion includes much from the confessions of the Reformed tradition. At times, he seems to treat his confessional tradition much as Rome treats the magisterium of the Roman church. "To understand how baptism relates to covenant, we must delve further into Westminster's theology," he claims (p. 64). Surely "Westminster" is not a coauthority with Scripture. It provides us with interpretive possibilities in a large number of doctrinal areas and may serve as a standard by which Presbyterian ministers are tested for ordination, but it cannot be treated as an authority in interdenominational doctrinal discussion. Though I have sober respect for the Westminster theological tradition, I do not believe that it is an authority or that it can explain something that the Bible cannot.

Pratt's intent, surely, is to show that the confessional expressions about baptism in that tradition mirror the biblical teaching. Herein lies another area in which he seems to have assumed too much. After quoting several Bible passages that speak of baptism and salvation, he remarks, "These and many other NT passages seem to indicate that baptism is much more than a symbol. In the language of the Bible, spiritual realities such as rebirth, renewal, forgiveness, salvation, and union with Christ are intimately associated with the rite of baptism" (p. 61).

Whether such spiritual realities are "intimately associated with the rite of baptism" depends entirely on what one means by "associated." If union with Christ and all the spiritual benefits derived from this union are seen as pictured symbolically in baptism, then certainly we can agree that they are so associated. If he means that these spiritual realities are somehow communicated in baptism, that is not self-evident in the class of texts to which he refers.

Pratt does not argue that his understanding of these passages is correct but only illustrates that the Reformed tradition has room for this mysterious possibility of the efficacy of baptism. For example, the assumption that the "washing of rebirth" (Titus 3:5) refers to baptism is purely gratuitous. This text and several others that mention washing, cleansing, and water (e.g., Eph. 5:26; John 3:3–8) form a part of every sacramentalist's discussion of the operations of grace within baptism. None of them, however, even mention baptism. The reference to water and cleansing is much more easily understood in its canonical context of the use of water as a symbol of purification in the ceremonial law. These types of purification are then fulfilled in the personal work of the Holy Spirit in regeneration. Thus, the "washing of rebirth" should be read as "the washing which is rebirth, even the renewal of the Holy Spirit." This is a fulfillment of the prophecy of Ezekiel 36:25–27: "I will sprinkle clean water on you, and you will be clean; I will cleanse you from all your impurities and from all your idols. I will give you a new heart and put a new spirit in you;... And I will put my Spirit in you and move you to follow my decrees." This prophecy in turn gives the spiritual reality behind the series of ritual cleansings required of the cleansed leper in Leviticus 14:7–9, as well as other ceremonial cleansings. The fulfillment of such cleansings is not baptism but the reality of the operations of the Spirit in regeneration and sanctification.

This approach to sacramentalist theology is more confusing than it is spiritually mysterious. Pratt says that "spiritual realities occur in conjunction with baptism" (p. 61), but he lacks certainty as to how or even whether they actually occur. More confusing, and even disturbing, is his contention that "Reformed theology's emphasis on divine sovereignty and freedom leaves room for the sacraments to work in unexpected ways" (p. 63). From his discussion we are led to believe that we really do not know what the sacraments mean, what they convey, when they might transport sacramental grace and when they might not. This appears to communicate a nominalistic view of divine freedom, so that God might sovereignly decide not to keep any promises "intimately associated" with this sacrament. This is tantamount to an admission that nothing truly congruent with the divine character and the reconciliation of sinners to God, nothing necessary to that transaction, is present in the sacraments. Why, then, does Pratt want to reserve an aura of gracious power for what is purely a positive institution and may not operate in accordance with its supposed biblical purpose?

The indecision and lack of resolution is powerfully demonstrated in his contentions that "baptism and 'grace and salvation' are not utterly inseparable," that "it is possible for a person to be regenerated or saved without baptism," and that "not everyone who is baptized is certainly regenerated" (p. 63). We are forced to ask, "Is there any other aspect of ostensibly saving grace that operates in such an inconsistent manner or that cannot be relied on to accomplish its stated purpose?"

Part of the confusion seems to rest in Pratt's view that one symbol is fulfilled by another symbol. "It is evident from the Gospels," he believes, "that the Lord's Supper is the fulfillment of the rite of Passover" (p. 66). In the same way he asserts, using the Belgic Confession as his authority that "Reformed theologians and commentators typically focus on baptism as an initiation into covenant by pointing out a similar analogy between baptism and circumcision." The problem here is that the Passover is not fulfilled in the Lord's Supper, nor is circumcision fulfilled in baptism. The Passover finds its antitype in the death of Christ (cf. 1 Cor. 5:7), and circumcision is fulfilled in regeneration (cf. Phil. 3:3; Col. 2:11, 12). The Lord's Supper, then, as a positively instituted Christian ordinance memorializes the death of Christ. Baptism, as a positively instituted Christian ordinance also memorializes the new life as effected by the death of Christ. By his death he created the new-covenant community, a community in which circumcision of heart produces people "who worship by the Spirit of God, who glory in Christ Jesus, and who put no confidence in the flesh" (Phil. 3:3).

Pratt's assumptions lead to a misconstruing of the council at Jerusalem. He contends that Christ left the question of the perpetuity of circumcision to be decided by the apostles as Gentiles came into the church. Accordingly, "At the council at

Jerusalem (Acts 15), the Christian apostles determined that circumcision would no longer be required of NT believers, and that baptism alone would suffice as the initiatory rite for the Christian church" (p. 67). The text, however, says absolutely nothing about their deciding that baptism would replace circumcision. Instead, the evidence of the work of the Holy Spirit in changing Gentiles' hearts to believe the gospel convinced the assembly not to lay that burden on them. The fact that God had "purified their hearts by faith" and that Jews were saved "through the grace of our Lord Jesus, ... just as they [Gentiles] are" (Acts 15:9, 11) sufficed as a mark of Gentiles' being the people of God. The cessation of circumcision, therefore, means that the new mark of the covenant is not physical but spiritual. The memorial of this new life by Christ's death—baptism—marks the point of entrance of the regenerated person into a new-covenant community of believers and gives the testimony of his conscience that this new life is his.

If infant baptism is as important in the new covenant as circumcision was in the old, how could a denomination not require it of their membership? Do they have a right to change God's ordinance? Yet Pratt states at the end of his chapter, "In recent decades, a number of Reformed denominations have encouraged all parents to present their children for baptism but only required that ordained officers of the church have their children baptized" (p. 72). Does this indicate a deep-seated discomfort as to whether infant baptism can actually be defended as biblical?

A final difficulty resides in Pratt's collapsing of the new covenant into old. He virtually destroys any distinction between the two, making a de facto observation a de jure practice. While it seems undeniable that the "visible covenant community of the NT remains a mixture of regenerate and unregenerate people who are baptized" (p. 69), it does not warrant the introduction of the unregenerate into community under mandate to reflect the qualities of the new covenant. According to his interpretation of 1 Corinthians 7:14, an unbelieving husband is part of the new covenant. When he says, "Even members of the new covenant are now threatened with eternal judgment" (p. 69), he contradicts the promises of the new covenant. The writer of Hebrews warns those who apparently manifest a work of grace ("after we have received the knowledge of the truth" [Heb. 10:26]; "after you had received the light, when you stood your ground in a great contest in the face of suffering" [10:32]) but now felt sorely pressed by persecution to reject what they had professed and return to identification with a people of the old covenant. There is nothing in the text that assumes the baptism of infants but everything that assumes that the writer is speaking to those who have made a credible profession of faith.

A LUTHERAN RESPONSE

Robert Kolb

That readers find many similarities between a Reformed or Calvinistic presentation on baptism and a Lutheran discussion of this "sacrament of the covenant of grace" should not be surprising. John Calvin often expressed his debt to the Wittenberg Reformers Martin Luther and Philip Melanchthon. He used Luther's catechisms and Melanchthon's dogmatic textbook, the *Loci communes theologici*, in constructing his initial editions of his monumental *Institutes of the Christian Religion*. Professor Pratt's analysis of the Reformed view of baptism parallels much of what Lutherans and others who believe in baptism as a means of God's regenerative Word would say about this sacrament.

Interestingly, as I note in my chapter, Martin Luther avoided the use of the term "covenant" to a large extent because it had been used by his instructors in the Ockhamist tradition of medieval Scholastic theology to talk about the sinner's ability to win God's grace by fulfilling God's covenant demands to the greatest extent possible. According to Luther's instructors, this fulfilling of covenant demands enabled the sinner to go on to earn God's favor, and ultimately heaven, through good works made pleasing to God by the addition of grace. Luther found the concept of a covenant a stumbling block for talking about God's grace and the human response to it. The exception was baptism, which he freely spoke of as a covenant received as a gift of God, a certain promise of salvation; and he could boldly state his confidence in the pledge that God makes in baptism.

When Pratt talks of God's covenant with his fallen human creatures in terms of two covenants, Lutherans are confused.

God's initial covenant is described in the Westminster Confession as a covenant of works, and Lutherans hear in this expression the assertion that human performance determined human righteousness initially and that the covenant of grace is an emergency measure designed to meet the situation created by the fall into sin. Luther's distinction between passive righteousness (the righteousness of trust) and active righteousness (the righteousness of acts of love) presumes that Adam and Eve were pleasing to God and regarded as his children only because of God's mercy, because God had decided apart from any grounds in them that they would be his own. God's expectations for human performance from Adam and Eve, their active righteousness, flowed from this passive, God-given righteousness that could not be earned by human merit. It was simply, also for Adam and Eve, a gift from his gracious disposition and the love for human creatures shrouded in the mystery of his divinity. God's covenant, Lutherans believe, always rests solely on that disposition and never, in any way, on human performance. This seems to be what the Westminster Confession (7.6) says when it states that there are not "two covenants of grace, differing in substance, but one and the same, under various dispensations." Lutherans believe that good works, new obedience in Christ, must flow from God's gift of a new identity as children of God, but they try to avoid the impression that human performance in any way ever contributed to our identity as the creatures and beloved children of our Creator. This seems to be Pratt's conclusion as well, despite talk of two covenants.

Lutherans place strong emphasis on "the means of grace," a designation for the uses God makes of his Word of promise, a Word that is re-creative, just as his Word in Genesis 1 was creative. It applies grace to believers, from a Lutheran perspective, just as Pratt describes the Reformed confidence in God's intention in giving his people this gift. Like the Reformed confessions do, Philip Melanchthon often described baptism as a "sign" in the Augustinian sense of a physical element that God uses to carry out his will.

Like the Reformed, Lutherans profess that how God works through his re-creating Word is a mystery. This divine usage of language as re-creative speech is more than what postmodern linguistic scholars call "performative speech," the speech that joins husbands and wives in a new legal and moral reality, or the speech that determines the future of the person the judge pronounces innocent or guilty. God does perform his will in bringing his grace and creating his relationship of Father to those whom he has chosen to be his children through this use of his Word in sacramental as well as oral and written forms. But human reason cannot master how the Creator works in this regard. Pratt's description of the mystery of God's baptismal utterance rings true to Lutheran ears. Reformed and Lutheran Christians alike view the sacraments and proclamation as two forms of the same Word of God that comes from Christ's death and resurrection as a promise.

Differences between a Reformed and a Lutheran view of baptism hinge on the framework for practicing theology and the presuppositions that give orientation for the proper understanding of what God is doing when he utters his baptismal Word through his church. Pratt writes that "the sacraments do not guarantee that their recipients will receive the blessings they offer" (p. 63). Lutherans agree that in the terrible mystery of the continuation of evil in the lives of God's redeemed people, some who have been born from above — who have been given the gift of being members of God's family through that new birth — do leave their homes, their families, their Father. Some may return when the ever-waiting Father (Luke 15), who sends out his good shepherd to hunt for the lost, retrieves them, but others die in the streets of a foreign city and do not return to the Father's table. Their unfaithfulness does not invalidate the promise God makes in his Word, however, whether it comes in a sermon, in conversation among Christian friends that conveys his promise, or in the sacraments. God is faithful, even when we are not (2 Tim. 2:13).

The problem that Pratt addresses is not just a problem with God's promise in baptism. The apostle Paul realized, after speaking of God's unconditional grace and mercy for three chapters, that some would ask whether they might continue in sin in order that grace may increase (Rom. 6:1). He had not been speaking of baptism in those three chapters. The problem with this kind of contempt for God's promise lay in the fundamental disposition of the gracious God who sacrificed his Son in behalf of the rebellious world of sinners. Baptism was, for Paul, the solution. The identity God had given his children in their baptism would not permit living apart from the Christ into whose death and resurrection they had been baptized (Rom. 6:3–11). God's gift of new birth in Christ brings with it parental expectations.

Therefore, Lutherans put God's baptismal promise to use, as they put all forms of God's Word to use, within the context of the proper application of the demands of God's law and the liberating promise of the gospel of Christ's death and resurrection. They indeed tell those who are stuck in rebellion against God and defiance of his Word that the baptismal promise and the nature of God as a gracious Father give no guarantees. But to bruised reeds and smoldering wicks (Isa. 42:3) they bring the assurance of God's faithfulness. This is not inconsistency in the Word of the Lord; it is a symptom of both the permeating nature of evil in human lives and the absolute power of God's love. Human beings live in two decisively and radically different realities: (1) in sinful defiance of their Creator and (2) in dependent trust in him who has come as Jesus of Nazareth to recreate them. These two fundamentally different types of human beings need two different words from God. The defiant must hear God's judgment if they are to be brought to repentance; the trusting must receive the consolation of the gospel that forgives sin and bestows life and salvation through Jesus.

Therefore, as Pratt affirms (p. 63), baptism is not utterly inseparable from grace and salvation. According to our Lord's command, baptism leads to teaching (Matt. 28:19) in the creation of disciples, and teaching helps the psychological aspects of faith, of the human relationship with God, mature. When this faith does not exhibit itself, Christians must be called to repentance once again. But for the disconsolate and despairing, God's promise in any form, baptism included, should be extended as the certain Word of the Lord, as a covenant he has made and will not abandon.

Therefore, this Lutheran is confused by Pratt's statement that, on the one hand, baptism is efficacious (p. 63), but, on the other hand, "Reformed churches do not baptize children to regenerate them or to remove the curse of original sin" (p. 70). Lutherans believe, too, that in the mystery of the continuation of sin and evil in the lives of the redeemed children of God, the original sin that consists of human failure to fear, love, and trust in God above all things, as Luther states in his Small Catechism, continues to plague believers. But they also are confident that God's Word of re-creation sets aside that original sin. God does not consider our sin, original or actual, but regards us as righteous for the sake of the Savior, to whose death and resurrection his word—given to us in baptism and other forms—joins us.

In my response to Professor Pratt's chapter, readers will identify at least two tasks for the ecumenical exchange between Reformed and Lutheran Christians. Our traditions, growing out of the same roots, have wandered apart into different terminological habits, and conversation can produce clarity on what we mean with common terms that are differently accented, such as "covenant," "means of grace," and the "efficacious" nature of baptism. Furthermore, we need more conversation on the way in which we practice the delivery of the Word of God to sinners, repentant and unrepentant. The practical aspects of the method of distinguishing law and gospel (which Lutherans find so valuable) might be a good place to begin that exchange, because ultimately both confessions desire to bring the living Word of God to the world of the twenty-first century.

A CHRISTIAN CHURCHES/ CHURCHES OF CHRIST RESPONSE

John D. Castelein

Christians in the Christian Churches/Churches of Christ will find much in Dr. Pratt's essay to agree with: (1) baptism in the NT is more than a mere symbol; (2) baptism unites believers to Jesus Christ; (3) there is nothing in the water that, in and of itself, regenerates the recipient apart from repentance and faith (this error is known as "baptismal regeneration"); (4) baptism works in conjunction with the preaching of the Word; and (5) "faith comes from hearing the message" (Rom. 10:17).

However, one concern is that Pratt's chapter relies so heavily on dogmatic interpretations of the Bible found in a variety of classical creeds. Without a doubt, readers who submit to the formulations of those creeds will find this essay persuasive and reassuring. It is true for all of us that anything that harmonizes with our general presuppositions (our worldview or paradigm) makes immediate sense to us, comforts us, and seems eminently true and valid. It is hard for any of us to break free from our own presuppositions or to persuade others to change their big picture of how salvation is accomplished. Christians who have been taught that the way to make mature disciples of Jesus is by first sprinkling them as infants will find it every bit as hard to change their paradigms as other Christians who have been taught that God in his sovereign grace allows sinners to choose life by intentionally and consciously committing to believe and to repent.

Reformed and Presbyterian theologies approach baptism

and salvation within the framework of an incredibly complex system of Calvinistic theological beliefs. In the end, they contend that the silence of the NT concerning the baptizing of infants must be interpreted as endorsing the practice. The reason is because God sovereignly has decreed that all his people on earth will live under one and the same covenant of grace. This covenant replaces Adam's original covenant of works that was in place before the fall. The Christian church of the NT in essence is the continuation of the church of the OT but with several changes that allow the Gentiles in mysterious yet real ways to share in the blessings promised to Abraham and his seed. One of these changes involves replacing the ceremony of circumcision, which brought infants into the OT covenant, with the ceremony of baptism, which brings infants today into the Christian covenant. It is claimed that this change of the initiation ritual was so natural and self-evident that it did not need to be mentioned, explained, or defended in the NT.

Alexander Campbell (1788–1866) was the primary spokesman in the nineteenth century pleading with Christians in the New World to leave their denominational divisions behind in Europe and to unite as "Christians only" under the authority of "the Bible only." Thus the Stone-Campbell Restoration Movement was born. Alexander Campbell, like his father, Thomas, came to America from Ireland in 1809 as a member of the Old-Light Anti-Burgher Seceder Presbyterian Church. He had been thoroughly trained in the Calvinist position of baptism of infants under the one covenant of grace. However, as he studied the NT, he came to understand that the church originally and intentionally immersed only penitent believers, able and willing to call on the name of the Lord.

As a result, Alexander Campbell engaged in three public debates with Presbyterian scholars John Walker (1820), W. L. McCalla (1823), and N. L. Rice (1843). He challenged them to determine the nature, purpose, and subjects of Christian baptism by working within the parameters of the definition of baptism given in the Westminster Confession (28.1): "Baptism is a sacrament of the New Testament, ordained by Jesus Christ." He simply asked to be given the NT proofs.

Four hundred and thirty years prior to establishing the Mosaic covenant of the law, God established in Genesis 12 his covenant of promise and grace with Abraham (Gal. 3:17–18). Circumcision is not mentioned until twenty-five years later when Isaac was born (cf. Gen. 17) and Abraham is a hundred years old. Now, it is absolutely true that in Jesus Christ, as Abraham's true seed, Christians are heirs to the blessings promised to the world through Abraham and his seed (cf. Gal. 3:6–29). Abraham, Isaac, and Jacob indeed are the root of the cultivated olive tree into which Gentile Christians have been grafted (cf. Rom. 11:13–32). But within God's one covenant of grace there are important discontinuities between the provisions of the Mosaic law—God's dealings with Abraham's physical descendants in the nation of Israel—and the provisions of the Christian church empowered by the Spirit of Christ.

From the outset circumcision was intended to mark males who belonged to the physical nation of Israel. Its restrictions were especially developed in the Mosaic law. All male infants born belonging to Jewish parents and masters (in the case of foreign slaves) were circumcised on the eighth day because they already belonged to Israel. This command was addressed not to the recipients but to their parents. It did not grant salvation but nationality and ancestry in a very special people whom God had set aside for the purpose of blessing the world through the coming of the Messiah from Zion. It is of vital importance never to forget that the same God of grace who made wonderful promises to Abraham is the same God who fulfills these promises in Jesus Christ. Even so, the church as the body of Christ stands in many ways in stark discontinuity with physical Israel while it fulfills God's vision of the spiritual Israel announced by the OT prophets (especially in Jer. 31:31–34).

As the writer of Hebrews explains, God himself found fault with the former covenant with physical Israel and declared it obsolete (cf. Heb. 8:7–13). That covenant was provisional until the Messiah would come (as Paul explains in Gal. 3:19–25). The Mosaic covenant with all its sacrifices, festivals, and provisions—including institutionalized circumcision first given to Abraham—was intended by God to reveal to his beloved people Israel that "all ... fall short of the glory of God" (even religious Jews; Rom. 3:23) and to prepare them to receive as their only righteousness before God the righteousness of the holy Messiah, Jesus Christ (cf. Rom. 3:19–31).

At the heart of the gospel, therefore, is the call for religious and irreligious people alike to repent (Matt. 3:2–11; 4:17; 11:20–21; Mark 1:15; Acts 2:38). God is not looking for more physical descendants of Abraham marked by outward rituals—he can create those from the rocks in the river Jordan (Luke 3:8). What God is looking for are people who, like Abraham, look to God in faithful trust (Rom. 4:1–17) and in obedient faith (Jas. 2:20–24) to be made righteous. He is looking for people seeking God's own righteousness, not their own self-righteousness (Matt. 5:6, 20; 6:33; Rom. 10:1–4). This righteousness that God longs for in his people involves a deeper circumcision than that of the male body; it is a circumcision of the heart (Deut. 10:16; 30:6; Jer. 4:4) that cannot be achieved by any human action except to allow the Spirit of God to wield the scalpel of his Word in the human heart (Heb. 4:12).

This is the shocking message Saul of Tarsus heard from Stephen in Acts 7:51: "You stiff-necked people, with uncircumcised hearts and ears! You are just like your fathers: You always resist the Holy Spirit!" When Paul in Colossians 2:11–12 uses the circumcision metaphor to describe how Jesus Christ in immersion "cuts off" his followers from the entire world, he is contrasting, not comparing, the inner circumcision of the heart, worked by the Holy Spirit, with the outer physical circumcision of the OT (Rom. 2:28–29). At the same time, he is also claiming that Christian baptism fulfills the inward circumcision God called for and promised in the OT prophets.

The continuity Paul sees between circumcision and baptism has to do with the way circumcision functioned in Abraham's life, but only in Abraham's life. Not for a single subsequent Jewish infant who was circumcised—because he was born under the law into the Jewish nation—did the sign of circumcision serve to seal a previous faith and trust in God's promises as it did for Abraham (Rom. 4:9–11). But if we walk as children of Abraham in the faith of Abraham, then there is a significant continuity between how Abraham's circumcision marked his separation from the world for God's cause and how our faith-based immersion marks our separation from the world for God's cause (Rom. 4:1–25).

The true circumcision Paul champions (Phil. 3:3–6) is not a matter of one's physical descent in the flesh (whether from religious or irreligious parents). What is needed is a new birth of faith, from above and from the Spirit, as the Word is heard (Rom. 10:17), believed, trusted, and obeyed. What makes one a true descendant of Abraham is choosing, as Abraham himself did, to trust God's promises. Thus the Christian believer is incorporated into Abraham's seed, Jesus Christ, by choosing to believe, repent, profess his lordship, and obey his commands—beginning with baptism (Gal. 3:26–29).

In short, circumcision in the OT was administered as a birthright to male infants for one reason only: they were already born in Abraham's natural family and already belonged to the physical commonwealth of Israel and would perpetuate its lineage until Messiah came. But Christian baptism of repentance and new birth is never administered as a birthright to anyone who already is in Jesus Christ. It is administered for the express purpose of marking the transferal of a penitent person who has come to faith in Jesus Christ from the kingdom of darkness into the reign of light in the church, the body of Christ (Acts 26:18). There is no merit, no credit, and no boasting for the person being obedient in baptism, but all glory goes to God's infinite grace offering forgiveness of sins through the death and resurrection of Jesus Christ!

Chapter 2: Reformed View (Richard L. Pratt Jr.)

1. See, for instance, Pierre-Charles Marcel, *The Biblical Doctrine of Infant Baptism: Sacrament of the Covenant of Grace* (London: James Clarke, 1953).

2. See G. C. Berkouwer, *The Sacraments* (Grand Rapids: Eerdmans, 1969), 27ff.

3. See Ronald Wallace, *Calvin's Doctrine of the Word and Sacrament* (Grand Rapids: Eerdmans, 1957).

4. See John T. McNeill, ed., *Calvin: Institutes of the Christian Religion* (Philadelphia: Westminster, 1960), 2:1023.

5. See Geerhardus Vos, "Doctrine of the Covenant in Reformed Theology," in *Redemptive History and Biblical Interpretation*, ed. Richard J. Gaffin Jr. (Phillipsburg, N.J.: Presbyterian and Reformed, 1980).

6. See Merrill C. Tenney, "The Gospel of John," in *The Expositor's Bible Commentary* (Grand Rapids: Zondervan, 1981), 9:135.

7. See William Hendriksen, "Exposition of Colossians and Philemon," in *New Testament Commentary* (Grand Rapids: Baker, 1964), 114–17.

8. See John Murray, *Christian Baptism* (Phillipsburg, N.J.: Presbyterian and Reformed, 1980), 6–30.

9. See Albrecht Oepke, "*Baptō*," in *Theological Dictionary of the New Testament*, ed. Gerhard Kittel and G. W. Bromiley (Grand Rapids: Eerdmans, 1964), 1:535–37.

10. See my "Infant Baptism in the New Covenant," in *The Case for Infant Baptism*, ed. Gregg Strawbridge (Phillipsburg, N.J.: Presbyterian and Reformed, 2003), 156–74.

11. B. B. Warfield, *Studies in Theology* (vol. 9 of *Works of B. B. Warfield*; 1932; repr., Grand Rapids: Baker, 1981), 9:408.

Chapter Three

LUTHERAN VIEW

God's Baptismal Act as Regenerative

LUTHERAN VIEW

God's Baptismal Act
as Regenerative

Robert Kolb

"Baptism ... saves" (1 Pet. 3:21). The apostle Peter was direct and simple. The waters of the flood through which God had saved Noah serve as the "type" or prophetic "representation" of what God was to do when he conveyed his promise to his people through his Word in baptismal form. As an "antitype," according to Peter's use of the terminology of the biblical interpretation of his day, baptism fulfills what God promised to his OT people. It gives salvation, that is, new life in Christ, to those "who have been chosen according to the foreknowledge of God the Father, through the sanctifying work of the Spirit, for obedience to Jesus Christ and sprinkling by his blood" (1 Pet. 1:2). Peter explained that baptism is no external kind of washing that simply removes dirt. It makes it possible for God's chosen people to stand before him with a good conscience. It does so through the resurrection of Christ (1 Pet. 3:21).

Peter did not write these words because he believed that baptism is some magical ritual but because he regarded it as part of God's re-creating, resurrecting conversation with his fallen human creatures. This baptismal action of God, which combined his Word with an external sign, was working in the fashion in which God's Word works in other forms as well. Like Paul, Peter believed that God has buried sinners with Christ Jesus through their baptisms and has thereby raised them to new life in him (Rom. 6:3–4; cf. Col. 2:11–15).

PRESUPPOSITIONS

Christians have interpreted Peter's words in different ways, based on differing presuppositions about the way in which God works within his creation and about the fallen human condition in a world rebelling against its Creator. Martin Luther held presuppositions that enabled him to understand literally the words of Peter and Paul, as well as Jesus in his conversation with Nicodemus (John 3:1–13). These assumptions led him to believe that God is working as the Creator of new creatures, as Paul calls believers (2 Cor. 5:17), when his baptismal Word begins, or renews, the conversation he always planned to conduct with his human creatures.

Luther's followers have maintained his view of the regenerating power of God's Word in baptismal form. They have recognized that Jesus defined baptism as an integral part of making disciples and commanded his followers to baptize in connection with God's action of turning people to himself (Matt. 28:18–20), as did the earliest Christians (Acts 2:38; 8:38; 9:18; 10:48; 16:15; 16:33).[1]

Other Christians have also professed, as Methodists did in their 1784 "Articles of Religion," that "baptism is not only a sign of profession and mark of difference, whereby Christians are distinguished from others that are not baptized, but it is also a sign of regeneration, or the new birth."[2] This reflects the position of the Church of England in its Thirty-Nine Articles of 1563. This document's statement on baptism reads as follows:

> [Baptism is] a sign of Regeneration or New-Birth, whereby, as by an instrument, they that receive Baptism rightly are grafted into the Church; the promises of the forgiveness of sin, and of our adoption to be the sons of God by the Holy Ghost, are visibly signed and sealed; Faith is confirmed and Grace increased by virtue of prayer unto God.[3]

Although Luther's colleague at the University of Wittenberg, Philip Melanchthon, had also called baptism a sign, he meant something other than did many who accepted the English statements. He believed that God's Word was at work with and through this sign. He summarized the Lutheran position on baptism in the Augsburg Confession of 1530 more simply:

baptism is necessary; grace is offered through it; children are entrusted to God and become pleasing to him through baptism.[4] Behind this brief statement lies not only Melanchthon's and Luther's understanding of what God does in baptism but also the place of this doctrine in the wider setting within the whole teaching of Scripture. My essay focuses on this confession regarding baptism that Luther and his followers formulated and that his followers continue to confess today.

Luther's teaching on baptism fits into a framework formed by several presuppositions. He presumed, first, that all of biblical teaching is a unity. He compared the content of Scripture to a body. This body of teaching functions as a whole, and one individual topic, subject, or doctrine can never stand alone, independent of other parts of God's Word for human creatures. Therefore, how believers conceive of God's action in baptism affects how they formulate other aspects of what they find in the Bible for their own use and the use of fellow believers. Likewise, the way we define other key elements of biblical teaching has ramifications for the understanding of baptism.

Second, Luther presumed that baptism is God's action, an action of his Word. As an OT instructor, he regarded God's Word as more than just information that points to heavenly reality. His understanding of Scripture caused him to regard the Word as God's actual instrument of creation (Gen. 1:1–31) and re-creation. Throughout the Bible, God was in conversation with his people, speaking to them through one prophet after another. The prophets conveyed more than information with their proclamation. Their word, as the Word of the Lord, made things happen: through it judgment fell and mercy was delivered. The culmination of God's revelation took place in the incarnation of the second person of the Trinity, Jesus Christ, whom John called "the Word [made] flesh" (John 1:14) and whom the writer to the Hebrews described as the one by whom God "has spoken to us" in these last days (Heb. 1:2). In the message that conveys Jesus, the gospel, God placed his power (Rom. 1:16), the power to forgive sin and to shape new life.

Luther believed that God enters into conversation with his fallen human creatures through his Word in oral, written, and sacramental forms. This Word creates faith and nurtures and strengthens trust as it comes in preaching and in the encouragement and comfort that Christians give one another. God's Word comes to his people authoritatively in Scripture, and from Scripture flow not only the various oral forms of the Word but also many written forms. In addition, God's Word comes associated with material elements that Christ placed together with his Word—in baptism with water, and in the Lord's Supper with bread and wine that convey the body and blood of Christ. In his Small Catechism, Luther asked the question, "How can water do such great things," such as forgive sins and deliver life and salvation? He answered, "Clearly the water does not do it, but the Word of God, which is with and alongside the water, and faith which trusts this Word of God in the water."[5]

Under the influence of the revival of Neoplatonism in Renaissance Europe, some of Luther's opponents presupposed that the material or finite order that God had created could not actually be used as an instrument to convey God's infinite power and effect his saving will. They believed that the spiritual is so superior to the material that God would not use selected elements from the material order as his tools. Under the influence of his instructors from a school of theology often labeled nominalism, which focused on the OT and emphasized the absolute power of God, Luther believed that God had been able to write the rules for his working in creation in any way he wished. Luther believed that God had selected human speech that transmits the work of Christ in the terms of the gospel to execute his plan for salvation and that the Lord had chosen to bestow the benefits of Christ's death and resurrection in sacramental form in connection with water and with bread and wine.

Third, Luther assumed that God's promise of life and salvation, in whatever form it first comes to a person, is an undeserved gift. Luther's entire theology arose out of his belief in God as Creator. Creatures cannot ask to be created, nor can they retroactively contribute to their creation. To Luther, this meant that "without any merit or worthiness in me" God created "me and all creatures," and that as the absolute, unchallenged almighty Father he had fashioned his human creatures without any conditions met or contributions offered from the human side.[6]

The same is true in re-creation. God's grace falls unconditionally on those whom he has chosen to be his own (Rom.

8:29–39; Eph. 1:3–11), and through his Word he brings forth those in whom he cultivates trust in him. For God did not make human puppets or automatons. He created willing and thinking beings, fully dependent on him, but in mysterious fashion, with an integrity of their own. This gift of new life does bring with it expectations, to be sure—expectations of performance according to God's will for his family. Fundamental among these expectations is the expectation of a relationship expressed in human trust and dependence, reliance and confidence in God—in other words, faith. But this faith and the new identity in Christ that God gives is a result of God's promise alone, not of any human action or merit. The good works of the Christian's life are the natural result, not the cause, of salvation.

Fourth, Luther defined sin as the failure to "fear, love, and trust in God above all things." He conceded that apart from the power of the Holy Spirit and faith in Christ, people can live upright moral lives and do much good within this world. They can fulfill standards of righteousness in their relationships within the horizontal sphere of life, that is, in relationship to other human creatures and the rest of God's creation. But righteousness in God's sight consists not in the performance of the deeds of the law but in trust in Christ, which is the gift of the Holy Spirit. Luther believed that the original or root sin of mistrusting and ignoring God permeates human life apart from Christ and that people are born with a craving for some other "god" than the true God. Therefore, he was certain that infants, who share the mortality that is the ultimate sign of sin (Rom. 5:12–21; 6:23), need the intervention of God, the new creation which his Word offers. He believed that this Word is given them initially in baptism.

Furthermore, it had become painfully clear in Luther's own life that the promise of God had ensured neither perfect faith nor perfect performance while life on this earth continued. He wrestled passionately with the remnants of sin and temptation that continued to plague him. In the Word of the gospel he found refreshment that sustained his life and impelled him to serve God by serving those whom God called him to uphold and support in daily life. His theology reflects this profound sense of the staying power of the spirit of rebellion and refusal that sometimes robbed him of the peace and joy of being God's child.

He rushed with sheer delight into the arms of the heavenly Father outstretched in the word of forgiveness extended in Christ. His monastic superiors classified him among those whom they labeled "scrupulous," too much concerned about their imperfections. It was this brutal honesty with himself, combined with the biblical text, that brought Luther to see the uncompromising condemnation of the law of God and the refreshing peace of the gospel of Christ.

This struggle with the mysterious continuation of evil within people who trust in Christ led Luther to see the entire life of the believer as a life of repentance, as he said in the first of his famous ninety-five theses.[7] Each day the Holy Spirit must turn God's chosen children from rebellion against him and rejection of his claims on them. He turns them into people who rely and depend on him and conform their lives to his plan for being human. Thus, Luther concluded his explanation of baptism in his Small Catechism with the question, "What is the significance of such a baptism with water?" He answered on the basis of Romans 6:4: "It signifies that the old creature in us with all sins and evil desires is to be drowned and die through daily contrition and repentance, and on the other hand that daily a new person is to come forth and rise up to live before God in righteousness and purity forever."[8] God's plan for human living, expressed in his law, continues to evaluate human performance on the basis of the demand that we mirror his holiness (Lev. 19:2). Each day this message brings us to repent. The gospel of forgiveness and life in Christ is necessary to restore the repentant to trusting God and obeying him.

BAPTISM AS GOD'S WORD OF NEW CREATION

In writing to the Romans, Paul first sketches the estrangement that has alienated even the pious from their God (1:18–3:20) and then presents the saving activity of God in Jesus Christ from several OT and contemporary perspectives (3:21–5:21). This rich detail regarding the good news of God's new creation of his own children out of fallen sinners raised questions regarding the mystery of the continuation of evil in the lives of the baptized. In Romans 7 the apostle treats the conflict within himself. At the beginning of chapter 6 he poses the question he knew would come from some readers: the King James Version so elegantly translates, "Shall we continue in sin, that grace may abound?" Paul's answer: "By no means!" This cannot be, according to Paul, though in this chapter he did not argue that this was so because God condemns sinners—indeed, he makes that clear in other passages (cf. Rom. 1:18; 2:2, 12; 3:5–8). His reasoning in Romans 6 rests on baptismal identity. He presumed that the identity of those justified apart from the works of the law (3:21–31)—who live by faith in God's promise, as Abraham had (4:1–25), who are righteous under the dominion of God's grace in Christ (5:19–21)—rests on God's baptismal action.

In essence, Paul's argument runs like this: "You cannot sin more because that is not who you are as one baptized into Christ Jesus!" (6:1–5). The apostle describes what God does in baptism as a twofold action: (1) he buries the sinner's identity in Christ's tomb, and (2) he raises up the baptized to "walk in newness of life" (6:4 NASB). Dietrich Bonhoeffer notes that "when Christ calls a person, he bids him come and die.... We do not want to die, and therefore Jesus Christ and his call are necessarily our death as well as our life. The call to discipleship, the Baptism in the name of Jesus Christ, means both death and life."[9] God bestows a new identity by his re-creative Word, on the basis of Christ's substitutionary death and resurrection. At the end of Romans 6, Paul notes that sinners must die (6:23a). There is no way around that. Sin pays a wage, and sin is an honest paymaster. It pays what is owed to those who have submitted to its lordship. All sinners die. They die eternally, or they die baptismally. For the latter there is a free gift, the creation of new and everlasting life (6:23b). Christ will not repeat his own death, and those whom God has raised with him in this baptism must regard themselves as "dead to sin but alive to God in Christ Jesus" (6:11).

The same description of baptism occurs in Paul's letter to the Colossians. There the apostle reminds his readers that they had received Christ Jesus the Lord and should continue to live their lives in him (Col. 2:6). In him, who has the fullness of the Deity, they had been restored to the fullness of their humanity (2:9–10). In him, Paul continues, the faithful have experienced a spiritual circumcision, which has put off the sinful nature. That is, the old identity as sinner has been eradicated and a new identity imparted, just as according to the covenant given to Abraham (Gen. 17:9–14) circumcision placed a baby in the community of Israel and bestowed an identity on him as one of the people of God.

This spiritual circumcision now takes place in baptism. There God buries his people and raises them up. He gives a promise to which the baptized respond, at the appropriate level for their age and its psychological development. When possible, this response takes form through the faith that is bestowed by the power of God that is lodged in his Word. This resurrection brings to a new life those who were dead in sins and "uncircumcision," that is, those who had been living apart from God and outside the community of his people (Col. 2:12–13). The forgiveness God gives on the basis of Christ's death and resurrection creates new life by "canceling the regulations of the law which condemns sinners," or by "erasing our past record" (both translations are possible) and by nailing the accusation of the law against us to Christ's cross (2:13–14). For Christ has disarmed the foes of his people and put them on parade, in the fashion of the victory celebrations of the Roman empire (2:14–15).

God creates a new identity for his people through this spiritual circumcision. This new identity makes a transforming difference in daily life. These newborn children of God are not subject to the same regulations regarding food, drink, and festivals as they had been; indeed, they are not subject to this world's governors and principles any longer (2:16–20). As the apostle observed to the Ephesians, those who were dead in transgressions and sins, living according to the passions and desires of their own waywardness, have been made alive together with Christ (Eph. 2:1–7).

Jesus himself commanded baptism. He instituted baptism as an integral part of bringing people into his kingdom as his disciples (Matt. 28:19). Coming under God's rule means forsaking a sinful way of life and being brought under God's fatherly, beneficent lordship. Christ spoke of this gift of the loss of our identity as sinners and the gift of the new identity imparted in Christ as a "new birth," or "birth from above." (Both translations of the Greek word *anothen* in John 3:3 are possible, and both are theologically apt.) When Nicodemus asked Jesus how a person can experience the kingdom of God, the Lord had a number of possible ways to describe how people come under God's rule. Given the Roman economy in Palestine at the time, he might have said, "It is like a business contract that is offered, which you must sign." He did not. He might have said, "It is like wooing a lover and seeking to gain her consent to marry." He did not. Entering the kingdom of God is not a matter of two sides coming to agreement. Coming under God's rule is not a matter of human desire or human willing. Those who receive Christ and believe in him have been given the power to become children of God from God (John 1:12–13). Therefore, Jesus compared coming to experience God's reign in his people's lives with birth (John 3:1–15).

Although babies cry and wiggle as they come from the womb, there is nothing more passive—more a gift—in life than being born. We neither asked our parents for the gift of life nor were asked by them if they could conceive and bear us. Mothers give birth, and children receive. God gives new birth, and this new identity is received by faith. This new identity involves trusting and loving the heavenly Parent who imparts new life. But he has made the first move, and he makes it independent of every condition on the human side of the relationship. The response of trust or faith results from, is not a cause of, God's re-creative act.

Although the biblical writers do not describe baptism as a covenant, theologians have designated it as such. Luther himself stated, "Baptism is an eternal covenant which does not lapse when we fall but raises us up again. If we fall out of the ship, God helps us on board once again. When Christians fall, they always remain in their baptisms, and God binds himself to them so that he will help them when the baptized call upon him."[10] When human belief asserts itself against the power of God's desire to save, the promise of baptism calls to repentance. Scripture never explains why some continue to resist and die separated from the God who loves them.

There is no satisfaction that merits baptism before or after the sacrament is administered. There is only the Lamb of God, sacrificed from the beginning of the world. He has the power to initiate life and to bring us into death.[11] Here Luther clearly did not understand the term "covenant" as had his scholastic instructors, as an agreement initiated by human works that had won an inferior merit in God's sight and led to his giving them the gift of grace: "No one can say [of baptism], 'I did this myself.' This covenant proceeds from God without our input."[12] Just as God had established his covenant with the Jews through circumcision, so his pact (treaty, covenant) between himself and his people is a promise that he will be our God and that he takes the infant who was circumcised or who is being baptized into his people as his own child. This covenant defines the baptized as God's children and as innocent. Christ functions as chief priest of the new covenant just as Abraham did of the old. Luther declares that with the new covenant in baptism, "God has established a covenant not just with one people but with the whole world."[13]

This understanding of a covenant ordained and put into effect by God corresponds to modern biblical interpretation of biblical covenants as conforming to the genre of the Hittite suzerainty covenant, in which the suzerain bestowed the covenant on his vassals.[14] Human creatures cannot force, cajole, or bribe God into a relationship with themselves. This relationship is always a gift, given without preconditions, simply out of the mercy that stands at the heart of his creative will.

Luther did use the biblical term "new birth" to describe what God brings about in baptism. According to Jesus, in his conversation with Nicodemus, this new birth happens through "water and the Spirit" (John 3:5). The Holy Spirit is at work through the water, but again, it must be clear, it is not the water alone that does it but the Word of God, the Spirit's tool, which is what is at work in bringing people into God's kingdom. It must be noted that although the word "baptism" does not appear in this passage, interpreters from the earliest exegetes of the church to some modern Baptist commentators (e.g., George Beasley-Murray) agree that "water and the Spirit" refers to baptism.[15]

Similarly, in his epistle to Titus, the apostle speaks of the "washing of rebirth and renewal by the Holy Spirit" that has changed the identity of the "foolish, disobedient, deceived and [those] enslaved by all kinds of passions and pleasures" into those who have received righteousness by God's grace and have become heirs who have the hope of eternal life (Titus 3:3–8). Born again and restored to their Edenic nature as children of God, his people live in that hope and "devote themselves to doing what is good" (3:8), as befits God's reborn children and brings goodness and gain to others.

Paul also presented this change of identity that the Word of God works, also in baptismal form, through the metaphor of dressing in Christ as a new garment. Those who have become heirs according to the promise, Abraham's offspring, no longer find their primary identity in nationality, economic status, or gender. They have become united in Christ through the baptismal word that has clothed them in Christ (Gal. 3:27–29).

Too many Americans are serious when they say, "I wish I were dead." Believers can bring God's forgiving Word to them that ensures new beginnings and fresh starts through the action of God. For adults, the oral Word that confronts them with Christ's promise of new life will soon be joined to the baptismal Word, as it was in Acts. God commands this, and our contemporaries need the expression that comes when water is connected with this promise. For he alone can lay aside our old identities and give us new birth as his children. Indeed, the newly reborn, like the newly born, need the help of more mature brothers and sisters in the process of growing and of living out each day. But the critical turn in life comes when God's re-creative Word, which makes all things new, proclaims a new core identity for one who had strayed far from God. In the mystery of the continuation of evil and sin in the lives of those whom God's Word claims, the battle will continue, as Paul related from his own experience in Romans 7, but God's turning is the decisive turn, the source of new identity through Christ's death and resurrection.

Throughout Christian history, baptism has also been described as a cleansing. The washing of water by the Word through which Christ takes away the spots and blemishes of sin prepares sinners to live lives of love for God and for others (Eph. 5:25–30). Luther found the comparison to cleansing weaker than the affirmation of baptismal death and resurrection, but it certainly speaks to those who are dealing with shame. For those who feel stained and soiled because of dirt splashed on them by others or because they have fouled their own nests with one transgression or another, God's cleansing power forgives sins and affirms that he loves us as individuals. That changes things. It makes a change that purifies and freshens. God's Word in baptismal form or in a reminder of our baptism drowns shame and washes away the feeling that we cannot stand where God or any other person can see us.

For those who seek escape from sin and evil in any of its forms the promise of cleansing or of a new identity in Christ brings liberation, a new beginning, a new sense of peace with oneself and with God. For those who trust Christ but are assaulted by doubt and discouragement, the gift of new birth is an anchor on stormy days and a comfort with which to combat the lies of the murderer (John 8:44). For those who want to have the gospel and go on sinning so that grace may abound, baptismal identity simply says, "No!" The baptismal promise of God has given us a new identity, with all the expectations that go with being re-created children of God.

BAPTISM CREATES COMMUNITY AND A LIFE OF SERVICE

Paul draws out the implications from this gift of new identity in the verses of Colossians that follow his confession regarding God's baptismal action in 2:12. Death and resurrection with Christ not only bestow God's gift of a new identity but also bring with it the expressions of that identity that reflect God's love for the world. In the continuing struggle against the remnants of sin within believers, Paul reminded his readers that they had "died with Christ to the basic principles of this world" (2:20). Dying with Christ has brought freedom from the oppression of systems for life that do not come from God. Believers "have been raised with Christ" (3:1), and this means that they are to set their hearts on things above. For, the apostle tells his readers, "you died, and your life is now hidden with Christ in God" (3:3). But the struggle continues, for they are to put to death sexual immorality, impurity, lust, evil desires, and the idolatry of greed—and all the sins that flow from them (3:5–9). This life possessed by those who have died with Christ and have been raised with him as new creatures (3:10) involves continuing to put to death what does not conform to the identity that God has given as children of God. For the Holy Spirit fosters in them a new character, typified by compassion, kindness, humility, gentleness, and patience—producing forgiveness, mutual forbearance, love, peace, thankfulness, and praise (3:12–17).

This practice of human identity as new creatures in Christ involves not only the performance of what God expects from those returned to Edenic listening to God's Word; it refashions the community God formed as fundamental to humanity when he observed that it was not good for Adam to be alone (Gen. 2:18). Being clothed with Christ in baptism means becoming part of God's family and Abraham's heirs (Gal. 3:26–29). The Holy Spirit has brought all of God's children together into one body through baptism, Paul told the Corinthians (1 Cor. 12:12–13). Jews and Greeks, slaves and free, have all been brought together by baptism into this new community, the family of God. In this community they serve one another, each with different gifts from the Holy Spirit for their common life as the servants of the same Lord, activated by God to function as a body.

This means that the baptized children of God can no more choose their siblings than any human beings can pick out brothers or sisters for themselves. God binds believers together on the basis of his choosing them to be members of the body of Christ and of the household or family of faith. They delight in the fact that some of them are to build up other members of the body by exercising the gift of wisdom, some with knowledge, and so on. In their new birth they find a common commitment to the common good under the guidance of the Holy Spirit. Their new identities express themselves in performing God's commands and fulfilling his plans for their lives as they love one another.

SUBJECTS OF BAPTISM

Lutherans believe that God wants all to be saved and to come to a knowledge of the truth (1 Tim. 2:4). Why some are saved and others are not remains an impenetrable mystery, according to Luther.[16] His "broken" teaching on predestination taught that salvation lies alone in God's choice of his people, a word of comfort, a word of gospel, whereas human beings must accept responsibility for their own rejection of God's lordship, a word of condemnation from God's demands for trust and obedience in the law. For those caught in their refusal to trust and obey God, the Word of forgiveness and reconciliation won by Christ in his death and resurrection comes to liberate. This Word calls them back into God's family as disciples.

Christ's command to make disciples by baptizing and by teaching (Matt. 28:19) does not prescribe a chronological order in coming into relationship with God. It does suggest, however, a theological priority. However, as new birth, baptism also points the way for maturing and growing in the faith, and this takes place through teaching. Both baptism and teaching, as forms of God's Word, transmit God's promise of new life, his pledge to be the forgiving God of the sinner who comes to faith.

Therefore, infants are given this promise, for they, too, show the symptoms and signs of the presence of the broken relationship with God. They can receive the wages of sin, namely, death (Rom. 6:23). They never grow up with a natural tendency to recognize God as their Lord and love and trust him; they need intervention from outside. Adults are dependent on the oral and written form of the Word when they come to faith, for they already have the functioning psychological components to respond with trust when God addresses them. So far as we know, infants do not. In both cases it is God who is establishing the relationship. In the case of infants, he does so with the promise of life won for them by Christ. In a manner beyond explanation, he expresses his promise to the infant through the Word in sacramental form, the Word of baptism.

Just as day-old infants are members of the family and receive the love of their parents, so those who cannot consciously respond to God's promise nonetheless are brought out of darkness into light by that promise in baptismal form. They receive the new life Christ has won for them in his incarnation, death, and resurrection. Parallel to the physical needs of a growing human being, they need nurture from other forms of God's Word. For they are still in the struggle against the assault of sin and evil from within and without. A part of this mystery of the continuation of evil in their lives includes the fact that they may later run away from the home prepared for them by their heavenly Father and die in the streets of a foreign city. Scripture does not tell us how it is possible that some run away in defiance of the God who wants all to be saved. But God's Word in baptismal form lays down the foundation of a relationship that he wants to last forever. In the midst of the struggles with their own sinfulness, believers can be confident that God's promise trumps its opponents, even though they know that sin rears its ugly, grasping jaws and hands to try to wrestle his people away from God. Thus, the conflict continues, but in Christ the victory has been won, the victory that he shares with those who are baptized into his death and raised with him to a new kind of life.

If sinners grow up apart from God and his Word and come to receive the promise through another form, in written or oral expression, they, too, should be baptized. But the baptism of adults presumes new birth through a word of witness, personally or through some electronic medium or form of print. Entry into God's kingdom presupposes repentance and baptism in Acts (2:38 and parallel passages); the Holy Spirit brings about new birth through the Word as it works on human creatures as God has created us, at the appropriate level of the use of our minds and hearts when he comes to us.

DESIRED MODE OF BAPTISM

Since it is not water that actually makes the life-giving difference in baptism, but the Word of God which is placed in the setting of the water, the mode of baptism is a neutral matter for Lutherans. Depictions of baptism from the sixteenth century indicate that early Lutheran baptisms in churches with large fonts continued the medieval custom of immersing the infants in their baptisms. In smaller churches, with fonts too small for such immersions, pouring of generous amounts of water provided the setting for the words of promise and new life. This latter mode has been predominant in most Lutheran churches and continues to be so today.

PRACTICAL ISSUES

Q: *Should people be rebaptized if they come from another perspective into membership?*

A: The promise of God comes irrespective of denominational membership. Therefore, when people have been baptized in the name of the Father, Son, and Holy Spirit in a community that confesses the Trinity, Lutherans believe that God has placed his claim on them, no matter how they may have understood or misunderstood what he was doing through his baptismal Word at the time of baptism. When people who trust in Christ come to a more complete realization of how God is at work, they need not ask God to repeat his promise in baptismal form; they need only the continued attention to the Word in other forms that helps the children of God mature as members of his family.

Q: *Should baptism be required for church membership?*

A: Since Jesus said that being born again of water and the Spirit is the way to enter the kingdom of God, baptism is a necessary requirement for church membership. Our membership in the church is not the result of a freely made decision on our part, as is membership in a club or team or political action group. It is God who calls people into his church, even when he brings adults into his family by acting on our minds and wills through other forms of the Word. It is God who gives and preserves the gift of faith. In addressing those old enough to understand, the appeal of the Word to repentance is a necessary point of departure for the working of God on hearts and minds that converts people from sinners to children of God. The apostles inextricably linked the working of God's oral word that produced repentance to the sacramental form of the Word in baptism (Acts 2:38 and parallel passages). Therefore, when he says that we are to be turned to him and to be baptized, this command creates the desire for baptism in the hearts of those who rejoice at being given the gift of life as his children.

Q: *How should we treat people who differ in their views of baptism?*

A: Differing views of baptism are like differences of any other kind among Christians. They are the occasion for gentle, respectful, sincere attempts to search the Scriptures prayerfully, alone and together, and to discuss how this part of the body of biblical teaching fits into the organic whole of that body. Those who look to God's action in their baptism as a gift of incomparable worth possess a joy that brings comfort and strength in the face of temptations to despair of God's love or to ignore this love by venturing into sin. Those who have experienced this joy, comfort, and strength want to rush into the lives of those we love. When differences in the way we read Scripture, out of differing presuppositions and assumptions, prevent us from agreeing, we expect Christian concern to share, in all humility, in a search for the truth.

Q: *How should candidates and families be prepared for baptism?*

A: Because baptism is not a magical act but is rather a new birth, candidates and their families need instruction in what baptism means for the newly baptized and those who love that person. Luther warned parents, with a very serious but ironically expressed observation, that they were making a lifelong enemy for their child when they brought him or her to the baptismal font. For the devil would engage in a never-ending struggle to win that child back to himself.[17] Those who are no longer infants, as they are about to be baptized, need to be fully aware of the implications of God's claim on them. For God's gift of new life comes with the expectations that that new life exhibits itself in trust in Christ and in obedience to his commands. Certain old practices and habits will no longer have a place in the newly baptized person's life. Certain new and exciting ways of enjoying our humanity through love for and service to other people and to God's whole creation become available. The strength and guidance of the Holy Spirit come to God's new child. But the struggle of the maturing believer is a real struggle, and this new child must be aware of the fact that attacks and trials will come.

The congregation needs to provide support for the newly baptized, both in the struggles against temptations to fall back into old ways of living and in the search for more information about this new way of life, which God gives through his baptismal claim. Even though in many ways the newly baptized will notice little change in their lives—they remain in their cultures, occupations, families, and so on—they have crossed a cultural divide. They have entered the culture of the church, a culture going back almost two thousand years, a culture set within other human societies around the world. God translates his message into all languages and cultures, but the newly baptized find that he transforms the people he calls to himself as he comes to them in their own cultures. The maturing people of God must give support for this cross-cultural trek to the newly reborn. Congregations should develop programs with specific helps for all new adult members so that they can integrate themselves into churchly ways of living, even as they remain planted in the callings that God has given them outside the church. There they must learn to be his salt and light; and for bringing the presence of God's love into home, occupation, leisure activities, and community life, they need training and assistance from seasoned Christians.

New parents have a variety of challenges in twenty-first century cultures, and for those who have a newly baptized baby in the family there are immediately thoughts of how to carry out the responsibilities of Christian parenthood. Congregations must give them support, first in the weeks immediately before and after the baptism, when they should receive instruction and encouragement as people called by God to the special task of raising children in the fear and admonition of the Lord (Deut. 6:7; Eph. 6:3), and then in the years following the baptism as children mature. For these years, parents need special help in fostering the maturation of faith through family devotions and conversations with their children regarding the faith, as well as through congregational instruction and edification.

Q: *Who is qualified to perform baptisms?*

A: Because baptism is an action of God, and because all Christians are called to use his Word to witness to their faith and to build up others (1 Thess. 5:11), Lutherans have always insisted that every Christian has the right to use God's Word in baptismal form in cases of emergency, where the life of a baby seems in danger and the parents seek the assurance of God's promise through the Word for their child.

However, coming into the family of God is a family affair, and so it should normally take place within the congregation in a worship service, where the pastor as a called servant of God and these people is acting on behalf of the congregation.

Q: *Should there always be preaching of the Word at a baptism?*

A: The Word of God is present by definition in every baptism, for baptism does not consist of water only but of water as the setting in which the promise of God is delivered to a new child of the Father. There may be situations in which threatening circumstances prevent any elaboration of what God has done in Christ for this new child. In normal situations, however, it is beneficial for the congregation in attendance at a baptism to hear more of the biblical message about God's coming near to give new life through water and the Spirit who carries the Word.

Baptism saves. It does not do so as mere water or as the cause of salvation, which lies in Christ's incarnation, death, and resurrection. Baptism saves as one form of the instrument God has used from the creation of the universe on, namely, his Word. He is a speaking, a communicating, God, and he established reality with his Word. His promise of life in Christ establishes the relationship with sinners that replaces all their idolatries and centers their lives on him. Therefore, as God's action, this promise delivered in its baptismal form creates and nourishes trust in God. This trust in the One who has buried our sinful identities in the tomb of Christ and who raises us up to live in Christ sustains faith, hope, and love for God and the neighbor in the believer's life.

A BAPTIST RESPONSE

Thomas J. Nettles

Many fine passages in Dr. Kolb's presentation describe the stewardship of life, as well as the privileges of grace that fall on the life of a person who is born again. All Christians should enter into this kind of encouraging exhortation. I find myself in agreement with virtually all that Kolb affirms on that issue. The one exception is his belief that the born-again person "may later run away from the home prepared for them by their heavenly Father and die in the streets of a foreign city" (p. 104). Not only does Scripture "not tell us how it is possible that some run away in defiance of the God who wants all to be saved," but it assures us of precisely the opposite. All who have experienced the reality of the new birth according to God's eternal purpose will most certainly be sustained according to his sovereign pleasure and grace (John 6:35–40; 10:26–30; Rom. 8:28–39; Phil. 1:6). Warnings abound of the most serious nature for all who have given some type of positive assent to the message of the gospel. They must examine themselves so as not to be found at last to have a wicked, unbelieving heart (Col. 1:21–23; 2 Tim. 2:16–19; Heb. 2:1; 3:12–19). These warnings constitute means by which the regenerate take heed, examine themselves, and persist in pursuit of true holiness. For a truly born-again person to fall away from the reality of the life that has been sovereignly and effectually bestowed would be for him to uncreate what God has created (Gal. 6:15) and to put to death what God has given indestructible life (1 Pet. 1:3–5, 23).

Kolb's view of infant baptism drives him to this assertion. When the magnificent gifts of salvation are granted to infants in baptism apart from their own cognizance, some mystery, un-explained in Scripture, has to be held as to why so many give no evidence of personal interest in biblical holiness and have no affection for the truths of the gospel. This is an end that cannot coexist with the nature of regeneration ("No one who is born of God will continue to sin, because God's seed remains in him; he cannot go on sinning, because he has been born of God" [1 John 3:9]), or the provisions of the new covenant ("I will put my laws in their minds and write them on their hearts.... They will all know me, from the least of them to the greatest" [Heb. 8:10–11]). Nor is it consistent with the care of the great Shepherd for his sheep, the purpose of the Father in giving a people to his Son, or the intercessory prayer of Jesus for those people.

A simpler explanation says they have not been born again. Infant baptism bestowed none of those transforming graces on them. That which was born of the flesh has remained flesh, and the pouring of water on a child who cannot hear the gospel with understanding and who has no conviction of sin and no faith in Christ has no biblical precedent for placing confidence in such a manner of making a Christian.

I mention only two reasons for my rejection of Kolb's, and Luther's, baptism scenario: (1) no instance of infant baptism can be pointed to in Scripture, and (2) we can point to no instance of salvation apart from the word heard. The apostle Paul declares that "faith comes from hearing the message" (Rom. 10:17). Kolb has sought to overcome this by asserting that God places the creative power of his word in material things, specifically the water of baptism and the elements of the Lord's Supper. He contends that this clearly manifests God's sovereignty in the granting of his gifts.

Such language has the enchantment of intriguing theologi-cal speculation, but compared to the biblical material it amounts to no more than an assertion. Passages that deal with divine sovereignty in salvation tie the intended salvation to the word, read or heard, and purposefully embraced:

> "... the word of faith we are proclaiming: That if you
> confess with your mouth, 'Jesus is Lord,' and believe in
> your heart that God raised him from the dead, you will
> be saved. For it is with your heart that you believe and
> are justified, and it is with your mouth that you confess
> and are saved." *Romans 10:8–10*

> And you also were included in Christ when you heard the word of truth, the gospel of your salvation. Having believed, you were marked in him with a seal, the promised Holy Spirit, who is a deposit guaranteeing our inheritance until the redemption of those who are God's possession. *Ephesians 1:13–14*

> But we ought always to thank God for you, brothers loved by the Lord, because from the beginning God chose you to be saved through the sanctifying work of the Spirit and through belief in the truth. He called you to this through our gospel. *2 Thessalonians 2:13–14*

Affirming the regeneration of infants through baptism amounts to an absolute imposition on the text of Scripture.

Kolb has helped me understand the philosophical assumption that allowed Luther to hold such a position. Although Luther's *Disputation Against Scholastic Theology* shows that he rejected many points of the nominalist school that formed part of his theological training, he also embraced it at some crucial points. In particular, Kolb points out the nominalists' peculiar views of "the absolute power of God" in accordance with which "Luther believed that God had been able to write the rules for his working in creation in any way he wished" (p. 94). By such an assumption, "Luther believed ... that the Lord had chosen to bestow the benefits of Christ's death and resurrection in sacramental form in connection with water and with bread and wine" (p. 94).

The nominalists rejected a view of the world that argued for a consistency between God's character and God's works of creation and redemption. They were skeptical, therefore, about the value of the cosmological, teleological, and axiological arguments for the existence of God. In addition, they believed that theoretically God could have required in his law that his creatures hate him rather than love him. He could have redeemed sinners, had he so chosen, out of his absolute power and uncircumscribed will, through a donkey as well as through the Son of God. By the same token, he decides that the waters of baptism will communicate the saving power of his word, though no intrinsic moral connection exists between such an action and the nature of God.

Though I would confess with Kolb the absolute sovereignty of God, including the trait of voluntariness in God's actions, I would suggest we offer no insult to God's sovereignty when we observe that all his works are consistent with his nature. When he wills to save, the salvation manifests the operations of his intrinsic holiness in a way consistent with the sinner's reflection of God's image. God cannot, therefore, accept our failure to obey his law as anything other than sin. His sovereign choice cannot make our sinful rebellion the material of our justification before him. As Paul declared, "I do not set aside the grace of God, for if righteousness could be gained through the law, Christ died for nothing!" (Gal. 2:21).

Nor can God be just in saving sinners without sufficient satisfaction to his honor and sufficient wrath actually falling on one who incurs legal debt for sin:

> But now a righteousness from God, apart from law, has been made known, to which the Law and the Prophets testify. This righteousness from God comes through faith in Jesus Christ to all who believe. There is no difference, for all have sinned and fall short of the glory of God, and are justified freely by his grace through the redemption that came by Christ Jesus. God presented him as a sacrifice of atonement, through faith in his blood. He did this to demonstrate his justice, because in his forbearance he had left the sins committed beforehand unpunished — he did it to demonstrate his justice at the present time, so as to be just and the one who justifies those who have faith in Jesus.
>
> *Romans 3:21–26*

God's justice required that propitiation be made if any sinner were to be eligible for forgiveness.

Every aspect of those things essential to salvation has moral connection between the character of God and the sinful creatures he saves. God operates through the holy influences of his Spirit to bring a new moral disposition to the sinner. His truth operates to inform and fit the mind for the right perceptions involved in such a change. And it is Christ, who is one in our human nature and is covenantally our representative, who dies to render satisfaction to God's moral character.

Nothing of this sort can be affirmed of baptism. Baptism was not an ordinance under the old covenant, and yet people were saved. Neither the sacrifices nor circumcision had anything to do with the moral transactions consistent with salvation (cf.

Ps. 51; Rom. 2:25–29; Heb. 10:1–14). Baptism, therefore, symbolizes the saving moral transaction of God but does not constitute any essential element of it.

Kolb has two theologies of baptism—one for infants and one for adults. He recognizes that "adults are dependent on the oral and written form of the Word when they come to faith, for they already have the functioning psychological components to respond with trust when God addresses them" (p. 104). Accordingly, they should not be baptized until that trust is evident. Without fail, this is what we observe in the NT. For infants, God establishes a relationship "with the promise of life won for them by Christ. In a manner beyond explanation he expresses his promise to the infant through the Word in sacramental form, the Word of baptism" (p. 104). This is "beyond explanation" because no word of revelation addresses it either in precept or example. Nothing can be said about it, because the NT neither records nor contemplates such a thing. The regeneration of infants through baptism does not exist.

A REFORMED RESPONSE

Richard L. Pratt Jr.

Dr. Kolb has presented a succinct and helpful summary of the Lutheran doctrine of baptism. Without a doubt, Lutheran and Reformed views on baptism are similar in many ways. In fact, one may say with confidence that the Reformed doctrine of baptism is closer to the Lutheran view than to the other views presented in this book. For instance, we both believe that baptism is more than mere symbol, but we do not see it as a necessary condition for salvation; we believe that baptism should be administered not just to those who profess faith but to their children as well. There are many levels on which we are in agreement. At the same time, important differences do exist, and these differences will be the focus of my reaction to Kolb's chapter.

On the whole, it is my opinion that the manner in which Lutheranism formulates its doctrine of baptism too closely associates baptism with saving grace. The Lutheran view does not utterly identify undergoing baptism with the reception of saving grace and clearly insists that baptism is not "some magical ritual" (p. 91). Yet, Lutherans describe baptism in ways that so closely associate it with saving grace that many evangelicals will wonder if their previous understanding of Luther's theology was accurate. Luther is best known outside Lutheran circles for championing *sola fide*, justification by faith alone. In my estimation, Lutheran teachings on baptism are compatible with justification by faith alone, but the Lutheran formulations so closely connect baptism and saving grace that important distinctions are difficult to see. In a word, from a Reformed perspective Lutheranism fails to distinguish clearly enough between baptism and the reception of saving grace.

To see how I arrived at this assessment, I will touch on four main issues: (1) the Lutheran tendency toward speculation in its formulations, (2) a failure to apply consistently the unity of Scripture to baptism, (3) a focus on the creative Word of God as opposed to the preached Word, and (4) an imbalanced outlook on covenant.

DOCTRINAL SPECULATION

By doctrinal speculation I simply mean that Lutheran formulations of the relationship between baptism and saving grace go beyond what the Scriptures teach. This tendency appears at the very beginning of Kolb's chapter when he asserts that the words "baptism ... saves" in 1 Peter 3:21 are "direct and simple" (p. 91). That is to say, they present no difficulty for Lutheran theologians because Lutheran theological presuppositions make them able "to understand literally the words of Peter" (p. 92).

In all fairness, the long history of debate among faithful Christians on baptism should lead one to suspect that NT texts are not as straightforward as Kolb's words suggest. I have to wonder how one can make such an assessment of the clarity of Scripture on this matter when well-informed Christians have taken such very different viewpoints. In fact, as Kolb himself suggests, it is the theological presuppositions of Lutheranism that make these passages seem so direct. Unfortunately, these theological presuppositions often are applied to matters that are at best speculative.

Herein lies one of the most significant differences between Reformed and Lutheran views. Reformed theologians generally insist that Lutherans go beyond Scripture in their attempts to clarify what the Scriptures teach about the relationship between baptism and saving grace. The distinction between Reformed and Lutheran views on the nature of Christ's presence in the Lord's Supper provides an analogy. Lutherans speak of Christ's presence under the rubric of consubstantiation. From the days of Calvin, Reformed theology has considered this explanation to be speculative and has described the presence of Christ as mysterious in an attempt to leave unexplained what the Scriptures themselves leave unexplained. In much the same way, Reformed theologians generally believe that Lutheran theology also seeks to define the connection between baptism and saving grace in ways that go beyond the teaching of Scripture. It would be difficult to imagine a Reformed theologian suggesting that the major NT passages touching on baptism are "direct and simple" or that we should take the NT "literally" in these matters. In a word, Reformed theology has been much more circumspect in its claims about the clarity of Scripture on these matters. This is why we stress the sacramental or mysterious nature of the relationship between baptism and saving grace.

UNITY OF SCRIPTURE

A second matter of concern from a Reformed perspective is Lutheranism's failure to apply the unity of Scripture consistently to the doctrine of baptism. Kolb rightly insists that Luther believed that "all of biblical teaching is a unity" (p. 93). This is true in the sense that Luther believed that every doctrine must be seen in the light of every other doctrine. In principle, we stand firmly with Lutherans in the belief that all teachings of Scripture form theological webs of multiple reciprocities. Proper views on the doctrine of salvation, God's Word, and the like inform a proper view of baptism, and a proper view of baptism informs these doctrines.

Nevertheless, Reformed theology is distinguished from Lutheran outlooks on baptism largely because we hold a more extensive view of the unity of Scripture, especially with respect to the unity of OT and NT teaching. Broadly speaking, Lutheranism has stressed discontinuity between the OT and NT under the rubrics of law and gospel. Reformed theologians see the OT and NT unified under the rubric of covenant and therefore see only differences in form and not in substance between the OT and NT.

This difference between Reformed and Lutheran views on the unity of Scripture comes to the foreground in Dr. Kolb's discussion of the relationship between circumcision and Christian baptism. At one point he says that "circumcision placed a baby in the community of Israel and bestowed an identity on him as one of the people of God. This spiritual circumcision now takes place in baptism" (p. 98). I find the referent of "this spiritual circumcision" unclear, but Kolb's discussion reveals a failure to acknowledge the unity of the OT and NT in at least one vital way.

Both the OT and NT differentiate between those who receive the physical sign of circumcision or baptism and those who undergo a saving "spiritual circumcision." Reformed theologians point to a twofold symmetry between physical circumcision that pointed toward the need for circumcision of the heart (regeneration) in the OT and physical baptism which points to the need for spiritual cleansing (regeneration) in the NT. Many who were physically circumcised in the OT were not inwardly circumcised. They benefited in temporary ways from their physical circumcision, but they remained under the eternal judgment of God. Only the inwardly circumcised in the OT received eternal divine blessings. In much the same way, many who physically undergo baptism in the NT are not inwardly cleansed and remain under the judgment of God. This distinction was very important to Paul as he ministered to Jews who relied on their physical circumcision for salvation rather than seeking inward circumcision (see Rom. 2:28–29). It should be equally important to Christian theologians now with respect to baptism because so many people trust their physical baptism to save them rather than turning to Christ in saving faith.

WORD OF GOD

Kolb argues that in Lutheran theology baptism is regenerative because it is "an action of [God's] Word" (p. 93). He rightly makes the point that in Scripture God's Word does not simply describe and command but often accomplishes things. On this matter there is certainly much agreement, but a significant difference exists as well.

Reformed theology has placed much more emphasis on the biblical connection between salvation and the reception of God's Word in the form of the preaching of God's Word, the Word of the gospel of Christ. This preached Word has creative power, but it also describes and commands. Kolb speaks of the Word of God in relation to baptism largely in the context of baptismal formulations or declarations associated with the rite. Reformed theologians have acknowledged the efficacy of the words of baptism but only as the fuller preaching of the gospel, with its long list of claims and demands, is received.

For example, consider Luther's formulation in his Shorter Catechism: "Clearly the water does not do it, but the Word of God, which is with and alongside the water, and faith which trusts this Word of God in the water" (p. 94). By contrast, Reformed theology more closely follows Paul's assessment of the process of salvation (cf. Rom. 10:14–17), in which baptism plays no explicit role. It is belief in God through the preaching of the Word or the gospel that saves, not trust in the "Word of God in the water." This is why we insist that it is possible (although it should not be normal) for someone to receive salvation through receiving the Word without baptism. In Reformed theology, the reception of the preached Word is the central focus, and baptism plays a distinctly secondary role.

COVENANT AND BAPTISM

At one point in his discussion, Kolb refers to covenant as a theological framework for understanding baptism. In this regard, the differences between Reformed and Lutheran views move to the foreground again. Kolb quotes Luther as saying, "Baptism is an eternal covenant which does not lapse when we fall but raises us up again. If we fall out of the ship, God helps us on board once again. When Christians fall, they always remain in their baptisms, and God binds himself to them so that he will help them when the baptized call upon him" (p. 99). Simply put, Luther spoke here of covenant in relation to baptism as an unconditional promise given by God to keep those who are baptized safe for all eternity.

This unconditional outlook on covenant faces serious problems in the light of the reality of apostasy. Experience and Scripture make it plain that not all who are baptized and wander from the faith are placed "on board once again." Unfortunately, however, the Lutheran view of covenant as unconditional leaves Kolb with a remarkable comment: "Scripture never explains why some continue to resist and die separated from the God who loves them" (p. 99). When Lutheran theologians assert that the phrase "baptism ... saves" in 1 Peter 3:21 is "direct and simple" and thus the baptized "always remain in their baptisms," it is no wonder that they have a difficult time finding a prominent place for biblical warnings about apostasy for those who have been baptized. A formulation of the covenantal character of baptism that has no explanation for apostasy will invariably lead many baptized persons to presume that they are eternally saved when they are not. This is the historical result for countless members of the church, especially in those traditions that too closely identify baptism with saving grace in their formulations.

The Scriptures speak many times about those who turn away from Christ, even though they have been baptized. The Reformed tradition has understood this teaching in terms of covenant by noting that covenant in Scripture is not a one-sided promise but a relationship that offers blessings to the faithful and curses to those who turn from the faith. Saving grace is not given to all who are baptized but only to those who have exercised saving faith that demonstrates itself in perseverance in covenant with God. As with circumcised unbelievers in the OT, baptized unbelievers in the NT age receive special measures of temporary mercies from God because they are associated with God's covenant. But only those who have saving faith receive eternal salvation, and God's grace will enable them to persevere in the faith. As a result, many who are baptized will fall away and will be left only with the certainty of eternal judgment. The writer of Hebrews summed it up this way:

> If we deliberately keep on sinning after we have received the knowledge of the truth, no sacrifice for sins is left, but only a fearful expectation of judgment and of raging fire that will consume the enemies of God. Anyone who rejected the law of Moses died without mercy on the testimony of two or three witnesses. How much more severely do you think a man deserves to be punished who has trampled the Son of God under foot, who has treated as an unholy thing the blood of the covenant that sanctified him, and who has insulted the Spirit of grace?
>
> *Hebrews 10:26–29*

In our day, many in the visible Christian church rely on a supposedly unconditional covenant promise associated with baptism and never come to true repentance and faith in Christ.

In such a circumstance, it is essential that we not allow the church to believe that baptism secures anyone's eternal destiny in Christ. We must call for saving repentance and faith.

I wish I could say that the issues I have raised in this response are of secondary importance. In reality, I believe they are at the heart of the Christian gospel, the gospel for which Lutherans and Calvinists have suffered much through the centuries. As central as baptism is to the doctrine of salvation, we must never allow anyone to rest his or her hopes for eternal salvation on the rite of baptism. I fear that while Lutheran theology as a whole does not support such an error, the Lutheran formulations of baptism often do just that.

A CHRISTIAN CHURCHES/
CHURCHES OF CHRIST RESPONSE

John D. Castelein

Christians in the Christian Churches/Churches of Christ will find much in Dr. Kolb's essay to agree with: (1) "baptism ... saves" (1 Pet. 3:21); (2) in baptism God works to make sinners new creatures (2 Cor. 5:17); (3) sinners will "die eternally, or they die baptismally" (p. 97); (4) baptism is an integral part of making disciples (Matt. 28:18–20); and (5) baptism saves because of the power of God's promises, not as a magical ritual performed on someone by the church.

My response will focus on the serious theological questions resulting from Martin Luther's continuation of the Roman Catholic practice of baptizing infants within the overall context of his Protestant theology of justification by faith only. I begin with the foundational Protestant belief that salvation is not in any sense a human achievement but results only from the actions of God, sovereignly and in his grace, acting as God on behalf of the sinner. Therefore, of the two ways to approach God—human works or human trust in God who works on our behalf—we are saved by faith and exclusively by faith. The great Reformer said that the best way to render Paul's exclusive claims for faith was the translation "by faith only."

For Luther this faith that receives justification from God is primarily individual *fiducia*, that deep trust in the heart that risks everything on the truth that God will keep his promises given to us in his Word, on the cross, through his Spirit, and "in, with and under" his two sacraments.[1]

Luther says that being saved is like an individual who must cross the sea: if he or she does not personally embark, salvation is not possible. In fact, without faith to trust God's Word of promise, the water is simply water and there is no baptism. Luther constantly stresses the indispensable presence of trust in the Word in strong opposition to Roman Catholic sacramentalism. In the Roman Catholic understanding, the sacrament of baptism brings about forgiveness merely by virtue of the fact that it is performed by the priest as the empowered representative of Jesus Christ. Baptism always infuses saving grace automatically, unless the person receiving the sacrament intentionally resists the grace at work in the act.

What is the content of this indispensable faith, the only human stance toward God that receives divine justification? According to the Christian Churches/Churches of Christ, faith is the acceptance of the biblical evidence or testimony that Jesus is the Christ, the Son of God. Therefore, in the Christian Churches/Churches of Christ we do not baptize anyone unless we first receive positive affirmation that this faith is present, through the person's voluntary and informed confession before witnesses (Matt. 10:32–33; 16:16).

In his own efforts to define the faith that saves, Luther sought to avoid two extremes: (1) baptismal regeneration as practiced in Roman Catholic sacramentalism, where infants are baptized on the faith of the church, and (2) abandoning baptism as sacrament altogether, as some mystics of that day were advocating. Therefore, he cast about valiantly for explanations to explain the presence of saving faith in infants. Until 1521, Luther had proposed that infants were saved by the faith of the sponsors at their baptism, but in 1522 he gave up the idea that anyone can be saved by the faith of another.[2] He also rejected the Waldensian position that infants are to be baptized on the basis of the faith they will develop later in life.

Luther next proposed that since God has allowed the church to practice infant baptism from early on—and the church has had many Spirit-filled leaders throughout its history—infant baptism must be pleasing to God. Therefore, we must assume there is faith in infants, even if we cannot explain it or give evidence for it. And, Luther said, this is really no different from baptizing adults who profess to believe God's Word, for who can know for sure whether their faith is genuine. In fact, Luther defended infant baptism on the very basis that the infant gives no evidence of having the rational capacity to hear the Word, understand it, judge it to be true, and embrace it as God's utterly dependable promise. He said that it was precisely their lack of reason that made children even better candidates for baptism than adult sinners, since adult reason always stands in the way of genuine faith. Luther is quoted as saying, "The less reason one has, the closer faith is."[3]

Luther's ultimate defense of infant baptism is summarized by Paul Althaus in these words: "What is decisive is that the Lord receives children and commands that they be brought to him. We baptize them on the basis of his will and word. Whatever the character of their faith may be, we leave it to him."[4]

In light of Luther's defense of infant baptism, it seems, therefore, fair to say that the content of saving faith for Luther, at least in these instances, is not the mind-informed and heartfelt trust of what God has done, and promises to do, for the sinner in Jesus Christ's death, burial, and resurrection. Rather, when it comes to infants, the content of faith consists of this: that their parents trust in what the church has preached and practiced throughout its history.[5]

Whether in its Lutheran or Presbyterian form, Christians in Christian Churches/Churches of Christ reject the practice of infant sprinkling because it is based on the underlying Augustinian premise that the only way to preserve God's sovereignty is to make saving faith from beginning to end a creative act of God. We do believe that God unconditionally and sovereignly chooses how he will save (e.g., through Jacob, not Esau [Rom. 9:11–12]), but we also believe that the invitation of salvation is genuinely extended to "whoever believes in him" (John 3:16).

Praise God that his grace has accomplished and finished our salvation in Jesus Christ! Praise God that his grace pursues us and invites us through the truth of his Word and the power of the Holy Spirit! Praise God that, though we are indeed dead in sin as far as saving ourselves goes (Eph. 2:1–5), God still invites us, in spite of our brokenness, to respond to and accept his offer of forgiveness and covenant life!

Praise God for the truth of Ephesians 2:8–9: "For it is by grace you have been saved, through faith—and this not from yourselves, it is the gift of God—not by works, so that no one can boast"! That which is called the gift of God in this verse (the pronoun "this" in Greek is neuter) is not the faith itself (faith in Greek has the feminine gender) but is the divine provision that grace offers salvation through the completed work of Jesus Christ, apart from any and all human striving, working, deserving, or meriting of God's favor. This arrangement is God's wonderful, mysterious gift of grace!

In this sense, we are saved truly "by faith only" and not by any human works! But such saving faith hears the good news of God's promised provision, understands it, judges it to be true, trusts it, embraces it, obeys it, and lives it with the help of the Holy Spirit.

SPECTRUM OF HOW BAPTISM FUNCTIONS

	Sacrament as channel of grace working apart from a recipient's faith	Sacrament as agent of God's (re)creative preached Word	Ordinance as occasion and ceremony marking formal allegiance	Sacrament as mystery, a sign and seal of the confirmation of the Spirit placing one within the visible church	Symbol and pledge of one's prior and saving faith	No function at all
Roman Catholic, Eastern Orthodox	X					
Lutheran		X				
Christian Churches/ Churches of Christ			X			
Reformed, Calvinist, Presbyterian				X		
Baptist, Anabaptist					X	
The Salvation Army, The Religious Society of Friends						X

Chapter 3: Lutheran View (Robert Kolb)

1. On the connection between repentance and baptism, see Frederick Dale Bruner, *A Theology of the Holy Spirit* (Grand Rapids: Eerdmans, 1970), 165–70.

2. John H. Leith, *Creeds of the Churches* (3rd ed.; Louisville: John Knox, 1982), 358.

3. Ibid., 275–76.

4. Philip Melanchthon, "The Augsburg Confession," in *The Book of Concord*, ed. Robert Kolb and Timothy J. Wengert (Minneapolis: Fortress, 2000), 42/43.

5. Martin Luther, "The Small Catechism," in *Book of Concord*, 360.

6. Luther, "Small Catechism" (explanation of first article of the Apostles' Creed), in *Book of Concord*, 354–55.

7. Franklin Sherman, ed., *Luther's Works* (Saint Louis/Philadelphia: Concordia/Fortress, 1958–1986), 31:25; *D. Martin Luthers Werke* (Weimar: Böhlau, 1883-1993 [henceforth *WA*]), 1:233.

8. Luther, "Small Catechism," in *Book of Concord*, 360.

9. Dietrich Bonhoeffer, *The Cost of Discipleship* (New York: Macmillan, 1959), 79.

10. *WA* 46:172.29–35.

11. See *WA* 46:172.12–17.

12. *WA* 27:33.27–29.

13. Ibid., 27:50.16–52.

14. George E. Mendenhall, *Law and Covenant in Israel and the Ancient Near East* (Pittsburgh, Pa.: Biblical Colloquium, 1955), 24–44.

15. See George R. Beasley-Murray, *John* (Word Biblical Commentary 36; Nashville: Nelson, 1999), 48–49; cf. his *Baptism in the New Testament* (London: Macmillan, 1962), 226–32.

16. "On the Bondage of the Will" (1525), LW 33:282; WA 18:785. 26–38.

17. "The Order of Baptism" (1523), LW 53:102; WA 12:47.21–29.

Chapter 3: A Christian Churches/Churches of Christ Response (John D. Castelein)

1. I have used primarily two sources in my response. Paul Althaus, *The Theology of Martin Luther* (Philadelphia: Fortress, 1966); Hugh T. Kerr, ed., *A Compend of Luther's Theology* (Philadelphia: Westminster, 1966).

2. I am dependent for all of this information on Althaus, *Theology of Martin Luther*, 364–65.

3. Althaus, *Theology of Martin Luther*, 366.

4. Ibid., 367.

5. Augustine once said, "I would not believe the Gospel if I did not believe the Church" (quoted in Kerr, ed., *Compend of Luther's Theology*, 13). Luther rejected any position that would subordinate the authority of the Bible to that of the church. Of those who used Augustine's statement to support that position, he asked indignantly, "What Scripture does he quote to prove the statement?" However, concerning the sprinkling of infants, Luther himself offers no Scriptures except for references to households believing the gospel in Acts and those Scriptures where Jesus welcomes little children who are brought to him to be blessed. Perhaps, in the area of infant baptism, Luther remained more of an Augustinian monk than he realized.

Chapter Four

CHRISTIAN CHURCHES/
CHURCHES OF CHRIST VIEW

*Believers' Baptism as the
Biblical Occasion of Salvation*

CHRISTIAN CHURCHES/
CHURCHES OF CHRIST VIEW

Believers' Baptism as the Biblical Occasion of Salvation

John D. Castelein

The yellowing card measures 6 inches by 4 inches. It is written in Flemish (what Belgium's Dutch language is sometimes called). It says that John Castelein was immersed in Genk (Belgium) on December 29, 1957, by Dominee Don Castelein. One corner mentions Ephesians 4:5 ("one Lord, one faith, one baptism"); the other corner reads, "Abide in Me, and I in you" (John 15:4). The bottom reads, "My sheep hear My voice, and I know them, and they follow Me" (John 10:27 NASB). It is signed and dated in my father's precise handwriting.

But eight years earlier, I had been sprinkled in a Roman Catholic Church near my parents' home. They hardly ever attended that church. I have no recollection of that first religious event. In fact, I wonder at times what effects that baptism may have had on my soul. However, I do remember vividly my second baptism. It was the eve of my turning nine years old. The otherworldly peace that filled the room where I slowly put on my dry clothes at times reverberates in me. I wonder how these two "baptisms" are related to each other.

Remarkably, the apostle Paul includes baptism in the short list of the seven basic realities that unify all Christians (Eph. 4:1–6). There was a time when the shared experience of baptism helped Christians to maintain "the unity of the Spirit through the bond of peace" (v. 3). Today, however, Christians give different answers to the most basic questions about baptism. Christians disagree on (1) the purpose of baptism (the why), (2) the recipient of baptism (the who), and (3) the mode of baptism (the how).

In this chapter I will try to present the answers given to these questions by two historically related, yet presently distinct, church bodies. Both fellowships consist of loosely connected nondenominational conservative churches. They are known as "Christian churches" and "churches of Christ," and both fellowships have roots in the "Restoration Movement" that originated in the early nineteenth century in North America with Barton W. Stone and Alexander Campbell. "Christian churches" are typically associated with the North American Christian Convention and two magazines, *The Christian Standard* and *The Lookout*. "Churches of Christ" have one primary distinctive belief: the NT does not authorize the use of musical instruments in worship services (thus they are committed to *a cappella* worship).

Neither of these church groups aspires to be a denomination or is officially structured as a denomination. Therefore, no one person or delegated group of people can represent their beliefs and practices in connection with baptism in any official or institutional manner.[1]

THE BASIC UNDERSTANDING OF BAPTISM IN MY TRADITION

The following is my summary of how the churches in my tradition understand baptism and the way it functions in the NT. Baptism is a religious act involving much water performed before witnesses. In this public act, God enters into a covenantal relationship with an individual, and, in turn, that individual knowingly and willingly accepts God's offer of restored fellowship.

In baptism God acts. God's sovereign act is to bestow on the repentant believer the spiritual blessings achieved by Jesus Christ in his voluntary sacrifice for our sins on the cross. We believe that in the NT plan of salvation baptism marks the point in time when God, because of his grace—and for no other reason—cleanses and forgives penitent believers of all their sins. It is the occasion when God incorporates them into Jesus Christ and instills his Holy Spirit in them. This divine transposition involves a dying to the sinful self and a rising up of a newly born person in Christ.

From the human side, an individual submits to a physical action in baptism. We believe it marks the time when the individual appropriates for himself or herself the promises of God's Word. The Bible tells us why a person wants to be baptized: because one hears and believes the gospel, because one puts one's trust in Jesus' death that atones for one's sins, because one desires to obey Jesus' commands to repent and to be baptized, and because one surrenders as an apprentice (disciple) to Jesus' authority and example. At baptism one renounces allegiance to sin and Satan and calls on Jesus' name as one's new Lord (the "Good Confession" or "Profession of Faith").

Maybe a good place to begin discussing our differences is the presumption that baptism functioned in NT times as the religious ritual that marked the beginning of one's allegiance to a spiritual Lord (i.e., it was an initiation rite).

THE MEANING AND PURPOSE OF BAPTISM

To discuss baptism's design we must first address the issue of how baptizing originated—most likely in the period between the OT and the NT.[2] Jesus himself pointedly asked the Pharisees whether they thought John's baptism came "from heaven" or was "of human origin" (Matt. 21:25 NRSV). Jesus probably wanted them to realize that even if the practice had historical roots, God in heaven still held them responsible for obeying John's call. Luke's gospel succinctly observes, "But the Pharisees and experts in the law rejected God's purpose for themselves, because they had not been baptized by John" (Luke 7:30).

As part of God's plan of salvation, baptism signifies both God's action and a human action. This divine-human interaction may be what Peter is getting at when he refers to baptism as "the pledge of a good conscience toward God" (1 Pet. 3:21). The Greek word *eperōtēma* (NIV, "pledge") is difficult to translate since its usage is extremely rare. When it does become more common in second-century AD Greek literature, it refers to the formal exchange of inquiry and answer by which contracts were ratified. Therefore, I propose that baptism signals an exchange of two promises. God interrogates a person as to whether he or she intends to accept the privileges and responsibilities of the promised salvation. In response, the person being baptized pledges what only an individual can vouch for himself or herself, namely, to believe, to repent, and to profess his or her new Lord throughout life.

We believe God's purpose in introducing baptism into history cannot be understood accurately apart from this holistic process in which the recipient, acting as a totally engaged individual, appropriates God's gracious offer for himself or herself. Strictly speaking, however, "process" may not be the best term to capture the reality of how faith, repentance, baptism, and profession of the Lord's name converge in responding to God's grace. God's own action (in ascribing Jesus Christ's righteousness to the sinner) presumably does not require a process in time but occurs instantaneously. The complete human response to grace in the NT, however, involves different human elements working together—which may require some time.

Now, this multileveled human response is what some Christians encapsulate under the single rubric of faith. But it is vitally important to understand that "saving faith" (defined that way) does not refer merely to mental assent to certain propositions. For the apostle Paul, for instance, faith is understood as involving understanding the gospel that is heard, trusting God's promises, and actively obeying the Lord's commands (cf. Rom. 1:5; 16:26). The entire NT, in fact, consistently unites faith and repentance as correlated actions.

On the other hand, the book of James appears to conceive of faith more narrowly in terms of mental activity not necessarily connected to active behavior. This is how James can make these remarkable claims:

- "Faith by itself, if it is not accompanied by action, is dead" (2:17).
- "Even the demons believe that—and shudder" (2:19).
- "[Abraham's] faith was made complete by what he did" (2:22).
- "A person is justified by what he does and not by faith alone" (2:24).

Working with James's definition of faith, in contrast to Paul's definition, salvation by "faith only" is simply impossible.

Understanding these nuances about how "faith" is used in the NT, Christian churches and churches of Christ see no tension between faith and baptism. Tensions and confusion result only when baptism is divorced from faith and then set over against it. Some Restorationist leaders view baptism as actualized faith and, therefore, see no conflict between baptism for the remission of sins and justification by faith. Internalized faith divorced from external baptism can become mysticism or Docetism (the idea that faith does not need to be historical and embodied to be real). External baptism divorced from inward faith can become mere ritualism.

BAPTISMAL REGENERATION

We believe that baptizing a person in situations divorced from that person's hearing the Word, trusting God's promises, repenting of sins, and committing to obey breaks this holistic faith response of the whole person. Also, it does not give public testimony to the fact that a person has chosen to embrace God's covenant. In fact, such baptizing constitutes the doctrinal error of "baptismal regeneration" or "water regeneration." The error of baptismal or water regeneration occurs when one believes and acts as if the mere performance of the ritual of baptism by itself saves. This practice assumes (wrongly, we believe) that the mere performance—apart from any evidence of personal faith, repentance, trust, obedience, and allegiance to Christ's name—forgives sin (which one has not repented of) and initiates a disciple-Lord relationship (which one has not consented to). Frankly, Christian churches and churches of Christ do not understand why anyone would charge them with practicing "baptismal regeneration" when they never baptize anyone unless that individual has confessed personal faith in Jesus Christ and professed him as chosen Lord.

For us, God's sovereign grace—and God's grace alone—is the grounds or cause of salvation (we are saved "by grace," according to Eph. 2:8). For us faith that comes from hearing the Word, that trusts God's promises, and that obeys his commands is the instrument or agency of salvation (we are saved "through faith," according to Eph. 2:8). For us baptism is the occasion and marker of salvation indicating in the NT that God forgives our sins and incorporates us into Jesus' death, burial, and resurrection (we are saved "in baptism," according to Col. 2:12).

These three distinct elements should not be divorced, confused, or interchanged. To make God's grace the agent of individual salvation removes all human responsibility to repent and believe (if one is elected and predestined, one will irresistibly believe). To make faith the occasion of salvation (seeing "faith" as the initial understanding and inner assent) undermines the biblical view of faith as the holistic response of the sinner that involves repentance, profession, and baptism. Genuine biblical faith asks, "What must I do to be saved?" (Acts 16:29), and then obeys the command to "repent and be baptized" (Acts 2:38; cf. Matt. 28:18–20; Acts 22:16; Gal. 3:26–27). To make baptism the cause of salvation leads to ritualism, legalism, baptismal regeneration, and meritorious humanism.

To use a simple analogy that may clarify this analysis, sin has resulted in an enormous debt before God that no human can ever cover by writing a check of good works. God's grace freely writes out the check for the full amount of our sins in Jesus' blood on the cross. Faith receives this check with completely empty hands (and even the act of receiving the gift of salvation carries absolutely no merit).[3] Baptism marks one's personal decision of endorsing for oneself on the back the offered check of forgiveness.

Because of its place in the conversion process as part of saving faith (defined here as the individual's total response to God's total act), baptism in the NT is repeatedly directly linked to salvation. Baptism explicitly is said to save by virtue of Jesus' death and resurrection (1 Pet. 3:18–22). Baptism will wash away sins (Acts 22:16; Eph. 5:25–26). Baptism in Jesus' name[4] and repentance are said to be for the express purpose of having one's sins forgiven and receiving the gift of the Holy Spirit (Acts 2:38–39).[5] Jesus saves us "through the washing of rebirth and renewal by the Holy Spirit" (Titus 3:5).

Christians today who wish to defend baptism's biblical role in faith's conversion process are hard put to find Scriptures specifically arguing for or defending baptism's role in salvation. The reason is simple: Scriptures do not argue for the penitent believer's baptism but *from* such a baptism since it was taken for granted that all believers started their life in Christ in baptism.

So, for instance, the apostle Paul in Romans 6:1–11 is not seeking to make the case that in baptism the believer is incorporated into Jesus' death, burial, and resurrection but arguing from this truth that the disciple should no longer continue to obey sinful desires.

SACRAMENT OR ORDINANCE

We usually refer to baptism simply as a commandment of the Lord Jesus. Most preachers will refer to baptism as an ordinance, but few of our preachers and teachers refer to baptism as a sacrament. Our reluctance probably stems from the Roman Catholic approach to sacraments. The standard definition of a sacrament refers to a ritual that channels God's efficacious grace automatically—independent of faith or repentance in the recipient. This automatic action is always performed, unless the recipient raises some obstacle to its working (stated in Latin: *ex opere operato non opponentibus obicem*). Christian churches and churches of Christ, however, have always refused to view baptism as a "procuring cause" (as Alexander Campbell called it) of salvation.

THE RECIPIENT AND REQUIREMENTS OF BAPTISM

How should we interpret the Bible's complete silence on infant baptism? Does it mean that infant baptism was taken for granted from the beginning, or does it mean that it was totally foreign to the new covenant being proposed? We take as our starting point something that we believe all Protestants can agree on. The essence of Christian salvation involves a person hearing God's promises and commands and responding in faith as belief, faith as trust, and faith as obedience. I have indicated already that if faith is defined as the total response of the whole person to God's offer of grace, we can agree with the Protestant position that all humans are saved by "faith only" and not by any work of merit.

The gospel begins with the surprising call, anticipated by John the Baptist and preached by Jesus Christ, that the natural-born children of Abraham need to repent. As Paul says succinctly, "For not all who are descended from Israel are Israel" (Rom. 9:6).

If God merely wanted more physical descendants of Abraham, he could create them from the rocks in the Jordan (Matt. 3:9–10), but God desires a new and spiritual Israel. This Israel will be made of believers born of the Spirit (John 3:3–8), having a new heart (Jer. 31:31–34; Ezek. 36:25–27) that is circumcised by the Spirit (Rom. 2:28–29), and intentionally walking in the faith of Abraham (John 1:12–13; Rom. 4:1–18; Gal. 3:6–18).

Baptism acknowledges that in my own human strength I cannot live a life pleasing to God (Rom. 3:23). It asks God to terminate my life "in Adam" and invites the Lord Jesus to live his life in me through his Holy Spirit (Rom. 8:10; Gal. 2:20; Col. 1:27).

When the Ethiopian eunuch asked Philip if there was anything that would prevent his being baptized, the early church supplied the answer: "If you believe with all your heart, you may" (Acts 8:37 NASB, not in the oldest manuscripts). We believe personal faith was universally the sine qua non requirement for baptism in the NT; therefore, we interpret the NT's silence on infant baptism to mean it did not occur.

It is true that as Christianity expanded in Western Europe, fewer and fewer adults presented themselves for conversion. Also, due to Augustine's teachings, parents became more and more concerned about original sin even in infants (especially given the high rate of infant mortality). So one can understand how infants historically in the West became the predominant candidates for baptism. But we believe this gradual shift in recipients represents a move away from the NT's norm of believers' baptism.

Sometimes we are told that dedicating infants in worship services and asking for God to bless and guide them (as we do) rather than baptizing them is the result of a mindless embracing of Western individualism. In response we contend that our actions result from the belief that God does not impute sin where there is no law (Rom. 4:15; 7:8; 1 Cor. 15:56). The apostle Paul explains that when he became old enough to grasp and become accountable to the law's demands, though he was "alive apart from law," sin sprang to life in him and wickedly used the good law to create sins (Rom. 7:7–13).

So we ask, in light of the evangelical gospel of salvation by grace through faith only, does not the burden of proof fall on those who seek to promote infant baptism as a genuine NT teaching and practice?

Some theologians have defended infant baptism as functioning in the same way circumcision of infants did in the OT. They give as evidence Paul's comparison in Colossians 2:9–14. The NT covenant does indeed have some things in common with previous OT covenants, since God instituted them all, but Israel broke that prior covenant (Isa. 24:5; Jer. 11:10). Therefore, more than comparing the two rituals, Paul is actually contrasting how much more radically Christian baptism cuts the disciple's entire body off from the world than the lesser cutting involved in circumcision. In Paul's theology it is actually the inward circumcision of the heart by the Holy Spirit that replaces outward physical circumcision (Rom. 2:28–29)!

Another proposed defense is the fact that Jesus loved and welcomed little children and urged his disciples not to hinder them but to welcome them (Mark 9:35–37; 10:13–16). But nothing in these beautiful texts speaks of baptizing infants—only that Jesus blessed them and commended their childlike openness to newness. Similarly, the fact that Peter mentions children in Acts 2:39 simply means the blessings promised to the believer's repentance and baptism will extend to them also when God in turn calls them.

What about the four "households" converted in the NT? We simply have no way of knowing whether there were infants in those households. Also, if there actually were infants too young to repent, believe, and profess Jesus' name, we don't know whether they were baptized at their parents' request. However, the attention in these passages is on those members of the family who were able to listen and receive the preached Word (Acts 10:33, 44; 11:1; 16:32), praise God (10:46), rejoice in the newfound faith (16:34), and devote themselves to the service of the saints (1 Cor. 16:15).

Are not children to be raised "in the Lord"? Of course. When both parents are believers—or when one parent is—the children are to be nurtured in Christian values and beliefs (Eph. 6:1–4; Col. 3:20–21). Such children are considered "sanctified" and "holy"—legitimate and acceptable to God (1 Cor. 7:14). But if we equate this being "sanctified" and "holy" with being saved by virtue of the believing family member's faith, then the spouse of such a believer would also be automatically saved.

Here is our real concern: With all due respect to the great Protestant Reformer Martin Luther, we submit that he was not able convincingly to reconcile the practice of infant baptism with his evangelical position on salvation by trusting God's Word only.

In further defense, it is sometimes contended that infant baptism, even better than believers' baptism, portrays the truth of the priority of God's grace to any human consent or activity. Now it is true that "while we were still sinners" — "powerless" and "ungodly" — God demonstrated his love for us. But he did that not at the point in time when an infant is baptized but at the time of the cross, when "Christ died for us" (Rom. 5:6–8)!

Yet those of us who practice believers' baptism must admit that our baptizing sometimes results in lives that are not Spirit-filled, in people who are not in love with God's Word or actively involved in holy living and joyful giving and worship. However, I think it is fair to say that infant baptism (especially indiscriminate infant baptism) may be the single most important reason why Western Europe is becoming lost to Christianity. Many potential converts to an active Christian faith have been rendered immune to evangelization due to their baptism as an infant in some church. I know this firsthand, as I was born in France and lived and worked as a missionary in my native Belgium.

THE MODE AND MANNER OF BAPTISM

Water is used for cleansing in almost all religions. The OT is full of references to water being used for purification and cleansing. Peter expected even those people who showed clear evidence of having received the Holy Spirit to be baptized with water (Acts 10:47). But how is the water to be administered in baptism? Can a little bit of water be sprinkled, or must more water be poured on the recipient? Does the person need to be immersed completely in water? Christian churches and churches of Christ (and even the Disciples of Christ) believe that baptism in the NT took place exclusively by completely drenching the person with water through immersion or submergence and that Christians should continue to perform baptisms in this manner today.

The reasons for embracing immersion as the sole mode or manner of baptizing strike us as clear and incontrovertible. We believe there is no question that baptism in the first century was performed by completely soaking with water the person being baptized. Along with Baptist Christians, we share some of the following reasons for immersing.

The first reason is the Greek vocabulary used. "Baptism" and "baptize" were not English words originally but are transliterations of the Greek noun and verb. In other languages where the Greek verb is actually translated, the words used all relate to terms for "deep" and "depth." *Baptizō* (the only term used for the ritual of religious initiation in the NT) derives from *baptō*.[6] The English meaning of *baptō* is "to dip." *Baptizō* builds on this original meaning of *baptō* but signifies repeated and intensive action ("to immerse, submerge, plunge").

The denotations and connotations of *baptizō* all fall in a clearly defined semantic domain: being completely surrounded with an element. *Baptizō* in the Greek literature can be rendered in many ways: "dyeing," "drowning," "dunking," "dipping" (as when washing), "sinking" (like a boat), "drenching," "inundating," "plunging under," "immersing," "submerging," and "saturating." Metaphorically it can mean "being flooded" (as with refugees), "being deluged," "going under" (as in debts or in an argument), "being engulfed," "being soaked," "perishing," and "being overwhelmed" (this may be why Jesus connects his baptism with his death).

Dictionaries of the Greek usage of *baptizō* show that a person wading through a river is "baptized" up to the waist, and a net is described as "baptized" while the cork holding it up is not. Naaman in 2 Kings 5:14 went completely underwater in the Jordan (one of the few occurrences of *baptizō* in the Greek OT).

There are good reasons for believing that proselyte baptism of Gentiles in first-century Palestine occurred by careful immersion (in the nude, with all rings removed and with a woman's hair loosened) to ensure complete wetting of the whole body. Likewise, all evidence points to the fact that baptism, as practiced by John the Immerser and among the Essenes at Qumran, consisted of immersion. In the few instances where the mode of immersion seems somewhat unlikely, good answers are available. For instance, Mark 7:14 makes us wonder if first-century Jews really immersed themselves before every meal and whether they really immersed their couches. But it may well be that only one's hands were dipped in water and that the furniture thoroughly washed involved either pallets or kettles and copper pots.

The second reason for holding to immersion as the proper mode for baptizing is that this kind of action best expresses the meaning it represents. Immersion represents so much more clearly—and more memorably than merely pouring water or sprinkling water on the head—the death, burial, and resurrection of Jesus Christ, into which the person being baptized is incorporated (Rom. 6:1–11; Col. 2:12).

The third reason is that Christian scholars across all denominations and churches (Orthodox, Roman Catholic, and Protestant) acknowledge that baptism in first-century Palestine involved getting the entire body wet by immersion. There are many supporting references to immersing found in the church fathers. Leading Protestant authorities agree, including Martin Luther, John Calvin, and John Wesley.

Finally, we can trace the emergence in church history of sprinkling as a secondary mode of baptizing that eventually replaced immersion in Roman Catholic practice. The *Didache*, a second-century Christian document, allows for pouring—but not sprinkling—of water but only when immersion (preferably in cold flowing water) is just not possible. For example, a man named Novatian (ca. AD 251) received an emergency baptism by having water poured all over him while he lay in bed, since it was feared he would soon die. Such an emergency baptism is called a "clinical" baptism (from the Greek word for "bed"). When Novatian was later elevated to the priesthood, there was much protest due to his unorthodox and incomplete baptism.

By the middle of the third century, the church father Cyprian was still reluctant to declare that sprinkling was as valid a mode as immersion. Even by AD 753, Pope Stephen II, while in France, was being asked by monks from Cressy in Brittany whether it was valid to sprinkle an infant on the head. There are later councils (e.g., Calcuith, AD 816) that insist that even infants must be immersed. For a long time in church history, people who experienced only this provisional "clinical" baptism could not partake of the Lord's Supper until they were fully immersed. In fact, it is universally acknowledged that sprinkling and pouring did not become officially recognized as alternative modes to immersion until the Council of Ravenna in 1311.

It strikes me that the present-day debate on baptism's proper mode is not about the meaning of the Greek term or about the imagery that the NT invokes for baptism. Rather it concerns to what degree it is still important today to preserve the full effect that the NT speaks of in terms of the whole body being drenched with water. The sprinkling position holds that the amount of water is not as important as the fact that at least some water is used. We cannot help but believe that Jesus' exact words expressly command immersing as the way to create disciples (Matt. 28:18–20), that he himself submitted to immersion, and that every reference to the mode of performing this ritual in the NT calls for the body to be completely inundated with water.

PRACTICAL ISSUES

Q: An immediate practical question emerges: *Should baptism be required for church membership?*

A: Theologically speaking, this question requires a twofold answer, as there is a universal church and a local church to be considered. We hold that anyone who believes in Jesus Christ, repents of sins, professes Jesus as new Lord, and is immersed in Jesus' name is thereby incorporated as a member into Jesus' universal body, the church of all times and places. However, we believe this incorporation makes one also a member of the local expression of that supernatural assembly.

Q: *How does one actually join a local Christian congregation—especially if one has not been immersed?*

A: Christian churches and churches of Christ have dealt with this question of the "pious unimmersed" from the first days they extended their plea for all believers to unite around the Bible only and to forgo denominational divisions. There have been three major responses to this question within the Restoration Movement churches: (1) there are those who exclude anyone who has not been immersed from local church membership and also from possible salvation (the "closed membership" position, which is strongly exclusivist); (2) there are those who would exclude anyone who has not been immersed from local church membership but either refuse to speculate on the eternal destiny of the unimmersed ("it's up to God alone as Judge") or hold some more or less strong hope for their salvation (this may be classified as a closed membership but somewhat more inclusivist position)[7]; and (3) there are those—almost exclusively the Disciples of Christ (Christian churches)—who would not exclude any unimmersed person from local church membership or from salvation but would nevertheless teach and practice immersion as their only mode for baptism (an "open membership" position).

Assuming that it is biblical and appropriate to have an official list of members, traditional Christian churches and churches of Christ usually proceed in this manner: The preacher discreetly ascertains from the person responding to the invitation to become a Christian (immediately following any Sunday morning sermon) whether he or she has already been immersed. If the person comes forward as a penitent immersed believer, the person seeking membership is asked, with the congregation as witness, whether he or she believes that Jesus is the Christ (Messiah). Many preachers also ask whether the candidate accepts Jesus Christ as his or her personal Savior and Lord. Upon a profession of faith, the "right hand" of fellowship is extended (Gal. 2:9) and the person is now considered a member of the local congregation.

If the person has not been immersed, he or she is asked whether they are willing to be immersed immediately in that same worship service or at an upcoming service. If the candidate requires further teaching and instruction, the profession of faith and church membership are postponed until more teaching can take place.[8]

Q: *How should Christians treat others who sincerely disagree on these baptismal responses?*

A: In general, it is safe to say, since Christian churches and churches of Christ have no denominational structures, that each church should follow the teaching and leadership of its elders. Anyone seeking to become a member of one of our congregations, or choosing to be a regular guest, should understand that the church will preach and teach what it sincerely believes to be the gospel message: that baptism is for penitent believers only, to be performed by immersion only, as part of the biblical pattern of conversion. In almost every Christian church there are people, like some wonderful couples in the church where I preach, who love many aspects of our congregation but simply find it difficult to accept the need for immersion. They are not yet members but are certainly more than just visitors. We love these folks and rejoice that they worship and serve with us.

There is much liberty in Bible school classes and small groups to study and discuss baptism in all its aspects. However, I know of a preacher on the mission field who lost a significant amount of his American support when a Christian church that strongly and enthusiastically supported his work decided to withdraw support because of his stance that baptism was intended by God to be subsequent to the conversion process.

Q: *Who is qualified to perform the baptism?*

A: This is not a question for us. Since we do not view baptism as a sacrament, it does not have an efficacious power that derives from the performer (an ordained priest) or from the ritual itself. Many of our baptisms are performed not by ministers but by believing parents, friends, or other church members.[9]

Q: *What about families of young children seeking baptism?*

A: These families need to make sure that the child has a basic understanding of why conversion is needed (the concepts of sin and repentance), how Jesus' death on the cross achieves our salvation, and what is expected of someone who is Jesus' disciple. They also need to make sure the child is not seeking baptism merely to please the parents or to join friends. Baptism should not be rushed into precipitously, but neither should it be postponed for no good reason. It is a good idea to have children write out their understanding of and reasons for being baptized so they can read it for themselves later in life when they may question whether they had the right motivation and understanding at that time.

The apostle Paul writes, "I have been crucified with Christ and I no longer live, but Christ lives in me. The life I live in the body, I live by faith in the Son of God, who loved me and gave himself for me" (Gal. 2:20). I want to end with two questions: Have I counted the cost of such a life in which Christ must forever increase and I must forever decrease? Am I willing to let the Holy Spirit duplicate Jesus' cruciform life in my existence?

A BAPTIST RESPONSE

Thomas J. Nettles

Dr. Castelein and I have much in common in our views of baptism. His argument against the baptism of infants and for the baptism of believers I heartily endorse. His argument for immersion as the single mode of the ordinance given by the Lord I also fully support. His care in distinguishing between faith as mental assent and faith as consent of heart and soul is also important. In addition, I support his understanding that the new covenant creates a new mark for the people of God—a "new and spiritual Israel" as it were, consisting of those "born of the Spirit (John 3:3–8), having a new heart (Jer. 31:31–34; Ezek. 36:25–27) that is circumcised by the Spirit (Rom. 2:28–29), and intentionally walking in the faith of Abraham (John 1:12–13; Rom. 4:1–18; Gal. 3:6–18)" (p. 136).

One point of disagreement concerns Castelein's view of baptism as the occasion of salvation. One difficulty relates to his failure to maintain his self-imposed distinction between the ground as grace, the agency as faith, and the occasion as baptism. In reality he collapses the agency and the occasion into one:

> "Faith that comes from hearing the Word, that trusts God's promises, and that obeys his commands is the instrument or agency of salvation" (p. 133).

> "Baptism is the occasion and marker of salvation indicating in the NT that God forgives our sins and incorporates us into Jesus' death, burial, and resurrection" (p. 133–34).

Castelein then states decidedly that these "three distinct elements should not be divorced, confused, or interchanged (p. 134)." In fact, *he* has "confused" these elements. His definition of faith includes submission to baptism as the aspect of obedience to God's commands. Faith and baptism are mutually dependent and inclusive. Because he believes, apparently, that regeneration is the result of faith, one cannot be regenerated apart from baptism. "It is the occasion," Castelein observes, "when God incorporates [penitent believers] into Jesus Christ and instills his Holy Spirit in them. This divine transposition involves a dying to the sinful self and a rising up of a newly born person in Christ" (pp. 130–31).

This is problematic because Scripture represents all spiritual obedience as subsequent to and consequent on the new birth. One cannot see the kingdom unless he is born again (John 3:3); that is, one cannot have his eyes opened to understand and embrace the realities of God's merciful actions in establishing a kingdom of the redeemed apart from the new birth. Since this is true, one cannot believe with the intent of obeying without having already experienced the new birth. Apart from the consummated operation of regeneration, therefore, one would not even desire to come to the baptismal waters as an expression of faith in Christ and dependence on his redemptive work.

The apostle John, in both his gospel and in his first letter, regularly represents the new birth as precedent to all Christian virtue, love, obedience, and faith: "If you know that he is righteous, you know that everyone who does what is right has been born of him" (1 John 2:29). The practice of righteousness is the evidence of, not the cause of or the occasion of, the new birth: "No one who is born of God will continue to sin, because God's seed remains in him; he cannot go on sinning, because he has been born of God" (1 John 3:9). Christians have an intrinsic revolt against sin and detestation of it and are no longer under its reign because of the new birth. The new birth caused their abhorrence of sin; their abhorrence of sin was not the cause or the occasion of the new birth: "Everyone who loves has been born of God and knows God" (1 John 4:7). Our love for God is not the cause or the occasion of the new birth. Rather, the new birth precedes, and this constitutes the source and cause of our love to God: "Everyone who believes that Jesus is the Christ is born of God,... for everyone born of God overcomes the world. This is the victory that has overcome the world, even our faith" (1 John 5:1, 4). Our faith that grasps the glory of Christ above all things in the world and that counts the world's applause and threats as nothing compared to the excellency of Christ Jesus manifests the presence of the new birth. Our faith is neither the cause nor the occasion of the new birth; rather, the new birth gives rise to faith.

For this reason, baptism follows regeneration, follows faith, and does not form a constituent element in either. All faith flows from regeneration; all obedience flows from faith. Baptism is an act of obedience to Christ that testifies to the prior existence of the regenerating work of the Spirit that has produced faith in Christ.

Though I mention elsewhere the concepts of water and cleansing as they relate to baptism, I will revisit it here. Those who believe in some sort of baptismal efficacy quote John 3:5 and Titus 3:5 as referring to baptism's relation to salvation. I don't believe that this assumption can bear scrutiny. In short, water and cleansing in these contexts refer to the efficacy of the Spirit-empowered word of God to apply Christ's completed work to cleanse the entire person of sin (its culpability, its corrupting power, and its reign). When Jesus spoke of living water as flowing from our innermost being, he referred to the cleansing power of the Spirit (John 7:39). Paul spoke of Jesus' giving himself up for the church, "to make her holy, cleansing her by the washing with water through the word" (Eph. 5:26). James, focusing on the word, wrote, "He chose to give us birth through the word of truth, that we might be a kind of firstfruits of all he created" (Jas. 1:18). Paul describes salvation in a monergistic context: "[God] saved us, not because of righteous things we had done, but because of his mercy. He saved us through the washing of rebirth and renewal by the Holy Spirit, whom he poured out on us generously through Jesus Christ our Savior" (Titus 3:5–6). He carefully constructs this presentation to exclude any act of human obedience, even relating justification in the next verse not to faith but to grace.

The author of the letter to the Hebrews discusses the ceremonial nature of washings to be fulfilled by the operation of God for his people: "This is an illustration for the present time, indicating that the gifts and sacrifices being offered were not able to clear the conscience of the worshiper. They are only a matter of food and drink and various ceremonial washings—external regulations applying until the time of the new order" (9:9–10). Later the same writer indicates that Jesus brought in this new order by his blood, "by a new and living way opened for us through the curtain, that is, his body, and since we have a great priest over the house of God, let us draw near to God with a sincere heart in full assurance of faith, having our hearts sprinkled to cleanse us from a guilty conscience and having our bodies washed with pure water" (10:20–22). The sprinkling of water and of blood has been fulfilled in the cleansing of the conscience; the "various washings" find fulfillment in the purifying of the entire life for the service of God so that we may present our bodies as living sacrifices and that the members of our bodies may now be instruments of righteousness.

These texts, along with others, show that the references to washing refer to the reality of spiritual cleansing as opposed to the OT ritual washings. These washings are fulfilled through the perfect, once-for-all sacrificial death of Jesus Christ by which he reconciled his people to God, thus gaining for them the Spirit's operations of calling, union with Christ, sanctification, and persevering grace. The washing of our bodies with pure water, being born of water and the Spirit, the washing of regeneration, the washing of water with the word point not to baptism but to the reality of the Spirit's powerful application of the word for salvation.

Those Scripture passages that verbally link salvation to baptism (e.g., 1 Pet. 3:21) I have already treated in my chapter. In summary, some passages deal with aspects of the immediate operations of God in salvation (e.g., 2 Tim. 1:9). In such passages we see three different aspects of the divine causation: God in his purpose and grace is the ultimate cause; Christ by his death and righteousness is the meritorious cause; and the Spirit by his calling and regeneration is the effectual cause. A second class deals with the appropriate and congruent human means and responses connected with salvation (e.g., "It is with your mouth that you confess and are saved" [Rom. 10:10]; "whoever turns a sinner from the error of his way will save him from death" [Jas. 5:20]). The third level concerns those reminders instituted by the Lord himself that all of our salvation resides in him and provides an ongoing testimony in the church of this reality. When our enactment of the ordinance reflects its reality, by metaphor it is said to save us: "This cup is the new covenant in my blood" (Luke 22:20), which is "poured out for many for the forgiveness of sins" (Matt. 26:28). Of this same sort is Peter's phrase, "baptism that now saves you also" (1 Pet. 3:21).

A REFORMED RESPONSE

Richard L. Pratt Jr.

Dr. Castelein has given us a presentation of the doctrine of baptism in the "Restoration Movement" that most evangelical Christians will find helpful, to say the least. After identifying the branch of the church in view, his chapter touches on six crucial issues: (1) "covenant" as the framework for understanding baptism; (2) the meaning and purpose of baptism; (3) the question of baptismal regeneration; (4) the terms "sacrament" and "ordinance"; (5) the recipients and requirements of baptism; and (6) the mode and manner of baptism, as well as some interesting practical questions. Many of these matters are not unique to his presentation and represent standard Baptist views on baptism. I will touch on three matters that set his discussion apart from a typical Baptist view.

BAPTISM AND COVENANT

Castelein rightly conceives of covenant in the Christian faith as two-sided—a divine and human activity. This two-sided outlook helps him avoid some of the pitfalls of other traditions. On the one side, because covenant between God and humans is an act of divine grace, Castelein argues that it is not appropriate to think of baptism as a meritorious work; whatever occurs in baptism is an act of God's gracious, unmerited favor. On the other side, however, Castelein rightly points out that covenants in Scripture involve human response to divine grace, human appropriation of what God grants in his mercy. Whatever we may say about baptism, it is not human merit;

it is nothing more than an appropriation of that which comes from the grace of God. By presenting this theological backdrop as he has, Castelein has effectively countered many of those who would accuse his branch of the church of treating baptism as a meritorious good work. Those who argue that seeing baptism as the occasion of salvation implies works-righteousness should be quieted by his explanation.

In this respect, Castelein's outlook accords well with Reformed theology. Although my branch of the church has stressed the necessity of obedience to the Word of God from those who have received the grace of God in Christ, we have always stressed that such obedience does not gain merit before God. Our obedience is, in fact, the demonstration of God's sanctifying grace that transforms our lives and brings us into conformity with the will of God. Although Castelein does not express his views by using these traditional Reformed terminologies, his basic outlook accords with that of the Reformed tradition.

FAITH AND BAPTISM, JUSTIFICATION AND SALVATION

Castelein makes a number of very strong points as he discusses the place of baptism in the process of salvation. At the heart of his argument is a threefold distinction that I find helpful in many ways: divine grace is the ground for salvation; human faith is the agency of salvation; baptism is the occasion of salvation. As far as these expressions go, there is little with which to disagree here.

Yet, serious problems arise with Castelein's definition of faith as he explains himself. In an attempt to develop a doctrine of faith that embraces both Paul and James, Castelein leaves the traditional Protestant doctrine of "justification by faith alone." To affirm *sola fide* in the sense of Lutheran and Reformed perspective, he says, "is simply impossible" (p. 132). He argues that faith includes understanding, trusting, and obeying. Thus, to say that one is saved by faith means that one is saved not only by understanding and trust but also by obedience to Christ— baptism being the initial step of such saving obedience.

At this point, it is important to clarify the Reformed (and, for that matter, Lutheran) position. In distinction from Roman Catholicism, the Reformers insisted not on "salvation by faith alone"; they insisted on "justification by faith alone." In the technical vocabulary of the Reformed tradition, justification is but one step in the process of the much larger category of the processes of salvation. Justification is that initial forensic declaration by God in which people passively receive the imputation of Christ's righteousness. It is a once-for-all legal declaration in the heavenly court, securing for all eternity the righteous standing of a person before God in Christ.

Salvation, however, includes not only justification but regeneration, repentance, faith, adoption, sanctification, and glorification (to name just a few). In this sense, justification occurs by faith alone apart from works of any sort (Rom. 4:6). A person is declared righteous before God solely on the basis of an imputation of Christ's righteousness when God's grace initially grants saving faith to that person. All subsequent good works flow into a person's life from God's mercy in sanctification and lead to glorification after that person has been fully accepted as justified by faith alone. Reformed theologians have always acknowledged that the Scriptures use these terms in different ways in various passages. This technical *ordo salutis* (order of salvation) has been based almost exclusively on Paul's use of the terms. Yet the distinction of justification by faith alone is a vital distinction because it safeguards against the encroachment of works-righteousness.

In this sense Castelein confuses matters when he takes "saving faith" to mean "the individual's total response to God's total act." Saving faith is not the sum total of what is involved in the salvation of a person; it is a person's initial response to the call of the gospel that places him or her in the condition of being justified before God. Everything else in the process of salvation either precedes or follows this justification by faith alone.

For this reason, it is no more appropriate to argue that baptism justifies a person than it is to argue that Abraham was justified by circumcision. As Paul forcefully argues in Romans 4, Abraham was declared righteous before he was circumcised. His standing before God was set in place before he was circumcised. In the same way, Christians are declared righteous apart from baptism. Their eternal destinies are secured by the application of Christ's righteousness to them apart from any good deed being performed, including baptism.

This is why the thief on the cross could be told that he would enter paradise with Christ, even though he had not been baptized (Luke 23:43) and why Paul was able to leave the baptism of so many in Corinth to others (1 Cor. 1:14). To put it simply, as important as baptism is in the NT for the doctrine of salvation, it is not necessary for justification.

We should grant that sanctification (the process of living by God's Spirit throughout life) is a necessary dimension of salvation. The writer of Hebrews makes it clear that "without holiness no one will see the Lord" (Heb. 12:14). We should also grant that baptism is a central act of obedience to be observed by those who are in Christ. Yet the list of holy acts that are necessary for salvation in this broad sense is very long, involving all kinds of holy activities. Baptism is not unique in this regard. It is but one of many things that faithful believers are to do to demonstrate the grace of God at work in their lives. Yet baptism and all these other acts of sanctification are the fruit of regeneration, saving faith, and justification that secure our eternal destinies in Christ before we act in obedience, even the obedience of baptism.

We should applaud Castelein's emphasis on the centrality of baptism in the process of salvation in many respects. Many contemporary Christian communities see little need for baptism because they reduce the entire process of salvation to justification by faith alone. Such reductionism usually leads to a view that negates the necessity of obedience. The temptation to receive Christ as Savior without receiving him as Lord must be countered in the strongest terms. Castelein is right to oppose this error by asserting the importance of baptism (as well as other acts of obedience). Yet it is also true that to identify any act, including baptism, as the occasion of justification is just as dangerous. It leads invariably to the position of Roman Catholicism, viewing justification as a process of infusion extending over the entire life of the believer. This heresy denies the sufficiency of Christ's atoning work and justification as a free gift entirely apart from works.

INFANT BAPTISM

Castelein opposes infant baptism in the strongest terms. Most of his arguments reflect standard Baptist views on which I will not comment. I was surprised, however, that Castelein insisted that Luther (I suppose the same applies to Calvin) "was not able convincingly to reconcile the practice of infant baptism with his evangelical position on salvation by trusting God's Word only" (p. 138). No doubt, the Reformer was not able to present the case for infant baptism "convincingly" in the sense that everyone has been convinced. Yet it seems an overstatement of major proportions to say that infant baptism is unable to be reconciled with the "evangelical position on salvation by trusting God's Word only." Evangelical paedobaptists have no more trouble reconciling these two doctrines than OT believers had reconciling the call to faith and infant circumcision. One may argue that there are little or no grounds to seek such a reconciliation of the doctrines in the light of NT teaching, but many have been convinced that they are reconcilable.

The crucial difficulty in Castelein's rejection of infant baptism is not so much in his handling of household baptism or in the NT stress on repentance and faith prior to baptism. He also points to the apparent weaknesses of arguing from Jesus' attitude toward children. In these respects, his arguments hold some weight, as all Baptists will argue. The most significant problem is his suggestion that "in Paul's theology it is actually the inward circumcision of the heart by the Holy Spirit that replaces outward physical circumcision (Rom. 2:28–29)" (p. 137). Hardly anything could be further from the truth. In Romans 2:28–29 Paul did not introduce a new concept belonging to the NT when he insisted that salvation comes to those Jews who were inwardly circumcised. This was the consistent teaching of the OT as well (Deut. 10:12–16; Jer. 4:4). Physical circumcision was never a saving ordinance. It was a covenantal rite that pointed to the need for inward circumcision for salvation in the OT. The paedobaptist argument is that baptism serves in the same way in the NT. Outward circumcision pointed to the need for inward circumcision; outward cleansing through baptism points to the need for inward cleansing. In my opinion, this line of reasoning against paedobaptism reflects a serious misunderstanding of OT faith.

On the whole, Castelein is to be commended for presenting a positive portrait of his tradition's doctrine of baptism. He has clarified the intent of the doctrine and how it fits within a view of salvation by grace. Yet his rejection of traditional Protestant distinctions and his misunderstanding of salvation in the OT lead to conclusions that have seriously negative ramifications.

A LUTHERAN RESPONSE

Robert Kolb

Professor Castelein provides a point of contact for Lutheran reaction to his chapter in his observation that Martin Luther "was not able convincingly to reconcile the practice of infant baptism with his evangelical position on salvation by trusting God's Word only" (p. 138). This statement reflects two things that strike a Lutheran reader immediately: (1) how much of what Castelein and I believe about baptism is expressed in similar (or the very same) language, and (2) how important presuppositions are for understanding how this language and the actions of both God and human creatures described by this language actually function in the lives of God's people.

We both agree that in the course of Christian life the human being whose psychological characteristics we can describe as active thinking and willing must repent of sins and trust in God as Creator, Savior, and Sanctifier. Castelein expresses this well when he says that "God in heaven still held them responsible for obeying John's call" (p. 131), and obviously all believers are among those who are held responsible for obeying what Christ commands. This obedience arises out of the teaching that follows baptism in our Lord's Great Commission (Matt. 28:18–20).

Furthermore, Castelein and I both agree that "in baptism God acts" and that "baptism marks the point in time when God, because of his grace—and for no other reason—cleanses and forgives..." (p. 130). The fact that Castelein completes the sentence with "penitent believers of all their sins" reveals, however, that there is a difference between our viewpoints. His wording implies that the human being comes to the event of new creation

154

and new birth in God's baptismal action with something that qualifies that person for the action of God. Indeed, the Bible shows us repeatedly that God holds his human creatures totally responsible for all that he has placed within our sphere of "dominion" or "rule" (Gen. 1:28) or responsibility. It also repeatedly affirms that God is the sovereign Lord of all his creation and totally responsible for everything that happens in it. He initiates everything, and he is in control, even when the evil that he hates and opposes breaks into his creation in the great mystery of human rebellion against the Creator. Christian theologians have struggled with how to harmonize or homogenize these two "responsibilities" that biblical writers presume as they talk about God and his human creature. Castelein seems to do so by looking to the human side first and presuming that the sinner needs to bring his or her penitence to the water in order to qualify for God's action.

Martin Luther refused to seek the proper proportions of divine and human action in the initiation of the relationship between God and his chosen people. Luther presumed that both human and divine responsibility must be taken seriously. The depths and full extent of what it means to be human is still a mystery to us, in spite of all we think we know about ourselves. Because Luther realized this, he recognized that we will never fully comprehend precisely how the creature made in the image of the Creator exercises this responsibility in relationship to the fully responsible Creator. That caused the Wittenberg Reformer to look to God's side first when he thought about baptism. It is precisely because of Luther's understanding that salvation comes alone, on the human side, through trusting in God's Word that he believed that God acts first and without condition—for no other reason than God's grace, as Castelein notes. God initiates, whether that initiation comes through baptism of the infant, who is subject to the wages of sin as a mortal, or through some other form of God's re-creative Word for a person old enough to be brought to faith through conversation with a Christian fellow worker, or through hearing a sermon on radio or television or tape, or through reading a Bible in a hotel room or finding a tract in a seat on an airplane or bus.

So Luther agreed completely with Castelein's description of the way in which God acts in our lives: "God's own action (in ascribing Jesus Christ's righteousness to the sinner) presumably does not require a process in time but occurs instantaneously. The complete human response to grace in the NT, however, involves different human elements working together—which may require some time" (p. 132). Because the Reformer viewed baptism as a new birth, or a birth from above, he believed that God's action and promise in baptism established a relationship, just as physical birth establishes the relationship of parent and child, even before the resulting psychological characteristics of trust and love are able to develop in a way that can be tested by human assessments. But just as parents expect their children to respond appropriately as they mature, so the teaching that follows baptism brings God's children to maturity in trusting, loving, and obeying their heavenly Father. This teaching brings them to meet the expectations of their heavenly Father, as Paul taught the Romans in chapter 6.

In Colossians 2:10–15 the apostle describes the death and resurrection produced in the baptized by their baptism as that which gives them the fullness of Christ through his cancellation of the written code, with its regulations, and his disarming the powers and authorities that oppressed his people. But in Romans 6 Paul uses the death and resurrection bestowed in baptism as the argument for their not being willing to go on sinning simply because God is gracious. The relationship God established in baptism is as sure as his Word is sure. But this relationship is also a human relationship with God, and from our side as human beings, it is a relationship of maturation. Luther wrote in the first of his ninety-five theses, "The whole life of the Christian is a life of repentance." For in the great mystery of the continuation of evil and sin in the lives of those whom God has claimed as his own, the battle continues against the law of sin within us. Day in and day out, the Holy Spirit is turning us back to trusting in our Lord and living in and for him.

This is why Luther refused to reconcile God's responsibility and human responsibility by homogenizing them. Instead, he held them in tension and brought each principle to bear on human life through his distinction of law and gospel. This method of using God's Word means that Luther shared Castelein's insistence that God's sovereign grace alone "is the grounds or cause of salvation" and that faith is "the instrument or agency of salvation" (p. 133)—although Luther agreed with some modern psychologists that trust is more than just an instrument but becomes the constitutive element in determining who we are. Luther also shared Castelein's insistence that repentance is necessary in daily Christian living. He rejected the ritualism of the church of his day that believed that mere performance apart from personal faith and repentance forgives sin. Baptism as human ritual action certainly is not the cause of the relationship between God and human being; the power of God's re-creative Word in baptism and in its other forms is. The Wittenberg Reformer did believe that God initiates our relationship with him and creates the new creature by acting apart from our preparation of ourselves, even though he requires in normally functioning maturing minds and hearts both that trust constitutes our side of the relationship with him and that this trust will produce obedience. Thus, God's action in his Word is primary. Its actual on-the-earth, in-the-middle-of-human-histories kind of power creates the relationship that blossoms into psychologically describable faith. This gives baptism, whether adult or infant, its fundamental significance for the Christian life.

Castelein rightly points to the question of why baptism sometimes, as he believes in his case, does not work (pp. 129, 138). The problem is not that of baptism alone, however. Apart from baptism, adult converts come to Christ and then fall away. This is a mystery that the biblical writers do not probe; they simply call all to come back to the cross. Just as a child who has run away and not enjoyed the benefits of his parents' home for many years will be sought and welcomed back, so God's promise in baptism can be a part of our call to those who have strayed from their Lord when we invite them to rejoin the family. Our abuse of God's promise does not abolish his promise, even though it invalidates its blessings for us.

The differences between Professor Castelein's and my presentations rest on presuppositions — in part methodological and in part at the level of our estimate of God's way of working and of the human obligation as defined by God's plan for human life. In actual application, it appears that Castelein probably operates with something like a Lutheran distinction of law for the unrepentant sinner who is fleeing from God, and gospel for the person broken by the effects of evil inside or outside his or her own mind and heart. The effective practice of that distinction is a difficult art to learn, but Lutherans believe that a conscious effort to distinguish the kind of hearer before us aids our delivery of the message.

In terms of interpreting the biblical message, we may differ as to our understanding of the depth of sin's permeating power in our lives. The effect of sin—death (Rom. 6:23a)—is present in all people, and no human child has grown up naturally knowing that Jesus Christ is Lord apart from God's Word as the Holy Spirit uses it (1 Cor. 2:14; 12:3). God's gospel—the announcement of death to our sinful identity and new life in Christ's resurrection—is not just a sign that points toward a heavenly reality. The Word of God as the gospel of Christ is his power, his instrument, for bestowing salvation (Rom. 1:16), just as his Word created the heavens and the earth (Gen. 1). Fruitful ecumenical exchange in our age can begin afresh by a common study of the presumptions that guide our reading of the texts that indeed point us in the same direction, even though we find significant differences in our address of baptism as a vital element in God's plan of salvation.

Chapter 4: Christian Churches/Churches of Christ View (John D. Castelein)

1. There is some overlap in the church names used. Some Christian churches that do use musical instruments in worship also go by the name "Church of Christ." There is no body of delegates that determines what these two fellowships believe. Local elders oversee the beliefs and practices of each congregation. The Christian Church (Disciples of Christ) represents the more liberal third fellowship in this religious heritage. The Disciples of Christ have become a denomination in their own right and will only incidentally be mentioned in this essay.

2. Precedents for understanding the mode and purpose of baptism in first-century Palestine usually include (1) Jewish proselyte baptism of Gentile converts, (2) possibly Essenic baptisms at Qumran, and (3) John the Baptist's baptism.

3. Contrary to some teaching today, the NT actually calls faith a "work" and does not call it a gift. When John 6:28–29 speaks of faith as the "work" that God would have us to do, Jesus is referring to the entire process of humans' receiving God's act of grace. Jesus' frame of reference is not any kind of work of merit by which a human merits God's forgiveness. In contrast, in Romans 4:5, it is precisely that kind of work of the law that Paul rejects as saving when he says, "To the man who does not work but trusts God who justifies the wicked,

his faith is credited as righteousness." Ephesians 2:8–9 teaches not that faith is a gift of God ("faith" in Greek is feminine but "this" is neuter) but that salvation by grace is God's gift to us.

4. In his Pentecost sermon, Peter quotes Joel's prophecy that anyone who "calls on the name of the Lord will be saved" (Acts 2:21). God has made Jesus both the Messiah of Psalm 16 and the Lord of Psalm 110 (Acts 2:36). Therefore, Acts 2:38 specifically calls on all Israel to repent and each person to be baptized "upon" Jesus' name (*epi* in the Greek). Repentance coincides with baptism and professing Jesus' name.

5. Baptism and repentance are both "for the forgiveness of your sins" (Acts 2:38). In the 1600 occurrences of this preposition [*eis*] in the NT its meaning is always purposive or consecutive (it expresses the intended result of an activity) except, possibly, in four instances where its meaning may be more nuanced. Matthew 26:28 uses the same purposive expression as Acts 2:38 to indicate the purpose of Jesus' death: "This is my blood of the covenant, which is poured out for many for [*eis*] the forgiveness of sins." No one would contend that a person should repent because God has already forgiven that person's unrepented sins. Until the theological innovation of the sixteenth-century Reformer Ulrich Zwingli, the church for over 1500 years unhesitatingly connected baptism and repentance with the forgiveness of sins.

6. The Greek language has specific terms for "sprinkling" (*rhantizō*) and "pouring" (*ekcheō*), and these terms occur regularly in the NT. However, they are never used to designate the kind of action used in the religious ritual of baptizing.

7. Some Christian church leaders believe that the only error concerning the mode of baptism that God in his grace may not overlook is when a person clearly understands that the NT teaches that baptism is by immersion but then refuses, out of loyalty to family tradition or out of stubbornness, to be immersed.

8. Strictly speaking, we do not consider this second ritual a "rebaptism." Many of the Christian churches I am familiar with do not treat a person who obviously loves and serves the Lord but has not understood about baptism by immersion as they would treat a lost person. We leave it up to God to judge the validity of a person's previous baptism if not performed by immersion. But like Apollos, who needed to be taught "the way of God more adequately" (Acts 18:26), we believe, teach, and practice immersion as the more adequate mode of carrying out Jesus' command to make disciples.

9. The point of 1 Corinthians 1:17 (where Paul says, "Christ did not send me to baptize") is not that the act of baptism is not important but that the person performing the baptism is not important. The passage shows just how crucially important the church considered the baptismal ritual to be in that there was even a danger of associating salvation with the person performing it. To combat this error, Paul forges powerful links that are not to be broken between the individual's salvation, baptism, the crucifixion, the name of Jesus Christ, and the unity of the body.

CONCLUSION:
FINDING COMMON GROUND
AMID DISAGREEMENT
AND AGREEMENT

John H. Armstrong

The purpose of *Understanding Four Views on Baptism* has been to provide a balanced and fair presentation of four distinctly different views of water baptism practiced within the Protestant tradition. To be sure, there are other views (and nuances of views), or at least different ways of stating or defending basic Protestant views. Within evangelical Protestantism alone there are modest (and sometimes acrimonious) variations of the four views presented here. As general editor I had to make several choices in addition to selecting the writers for the four chapters. The most basic was deciding which major views to include and how to frame the approach to each view. In the end the choice came down to four historically representative views that clearly lined up with the traditions and general practices common to our churches.

The topic dealt with here is worthy of an entire library of books, at least on one level. Indeed, the subject has generated countless pages of text over the centuries. My goal throughout has been clarity and simplicity, joined with respect and dispassionate fairness. I believe the four contributors have fulfilled this goal well.

In dealing with this complex subject we have sought to understand and answer the most basic questions. I am personally persuaded, after thirty-plus years of pastoral ministry and extensive teaching in seminaries and in conference settings, that the most important question remains clear: "What is the meaning and significance of baptism?" All the other questions addressed in this book flow from this one central question. Let me illustrate this point.

As you have seen, one of the more pressing questions in the baptism debate has always been, "Who should be baptized?" This is the question of the *subject* of baptism. The question comes to a point of significant disagreement when we state it this way: "Should we baptize only those who profess faith in Christ (i.e., Christian disciples who give evidence of faith and commitment to Jesus), or should we also baptize the children of Christian parents?" Our authors have shown how the answers vary considerably. Two contributors (Pratt and Kolb) would baptize the infants of Christian parents, but for different reasons and on a different theological basis, and two would not (Nettles and Castelein). This debate will clearly not be settled by these four presentations. But the presentations themselves can be used to shed a great deal of light on why different Christian churches do what they do with regard to baptism.

We have also addressed the issue of the mode of baptism. Again, the differences between each contributor are fairly obvious. What is interesting, however, is that even within several of the distinct traditions defended here there is some variation with regard to the mode question. Most are not quite as settled about this question as they were fifty years ago. Within the Reformed tradition there is a growing willingness to allow, and to actually practice, immersion. And within some Baptist traditions there is a readiness to accept those baptized as believers who were not immersed than there would have been prior to the last few decades.

A quick perusal of the relevant current literature on baptism reveals that the issue of mode and context is one that is plainly in some state of flux. Dialogue among various traditions has surely allowed people to hear other points of view and thus to alter what was once understood to be a "hard and fast" conclusion. Thankfully, mobility within our culture also forces churches to listen to people from other backgrounds in ways that would not have been possible years ago.

But I return to my earlier observation. The two issues, namely the recipients of baptism and the mode, are both inextricably related to the single central issue of the meaning and significance of baptism. How we understand the biblical-theological argument of texts such as Romans 6:3–4; Colossians 2:11–12; and Galatians 3:26–29 will ultimately determine how we relate to a host of other questions regarding baptism. The recognition of this one point will go a long way toward allowing those who disagree on various aspects of the practice of baptism to focus on the more important issue first, namely: "What does baptism mean, and why is it important?"

There are at least ten important things to say in conclusion to this discussion that I hope will guide you toward a deeper understanding of baptism and a fuller love for Jesus Christ:

1. We can and should believe that no one is warranted to neglect or denigrate baptism because there is disagreement among believers regarding its practice.
2. We can differ about the way in which grace and salvation are related to baptism without concluding that those in other traditions are without the grace of God because of this disagreement.
3. We can agree that not all who are baptized are truly regenerate and thus not all who have been baptized will be finally saved.
4. We can agree that baptism is not magic and that the application of the water of Christian baptism to a person in and of itself never saves them, which is the old danger of *ex opera operato*.
5. We can agree that baptism is commanded by our Lord Jesus Christ (Matt. 28:19–20) and thus should never be treated as trivial. Put simply, baptism is important, and this is why we must be serious about it: baptism is bound up with Christ and his gospel, and this connection makes it important for all who wish to be faithful to Jesus.
6. We can believe that baptism is a sign of Christ given to his people under the new covenant. It is the outward mark that is received prior to entry into the Christian church and still stands as a commandment for all who follow Christ. This will be so until the end of this present

age. By this mark we are set apart from others and from all non-Christian faiths and practices.

7. We can believe that baptism and the Lord's Supper are related to one another as blessings and benefits given by Christ to his church. We can also believe that baptism is to be administered once, while the Lord's Supper is to be administered frequently. Both of these signs nourish and strengthen our faith in Christ.

8. We can further believe (as Protestant Christians) that there are only two sacraments, or ordinances, given by Christ to his church—baptism and the Lord's Supper. Therefore we reject additions to these two and wish to practice only these two in a manner that will continually relate them faithfully to the gospel of grace. We should also reject all human innovations and laws imposed on believers from outside the Bible.

9. We can affirm that baptism in water, understood by means of the full teaching of the NT, is to be performed in the triune name of Father, Son, and Holy Spirit (Matt. 28:19–20).

10. We can agree that baptism is related to the redemptive work of Christ in the past, and thus we can see how it looks back to what Christ has done to bring in the "new creation" (2 Cor. 5:17), while it also looks forward to the consummation of all things in the coming of Christ in the future (cf. Rom. 8:18–25). In the words of contemporary Baptist writer George Beasley-Murray, "Baptism means hope!... Modern Christians would be strengthened by a fresh grasp of this aspect of the meaning of Christian Baptism."[1]

Having observed the importance of baptism, and the numerous ways in which we can and should agree about it as evangelical Christians, we must sadly acknowledge that we still disagree. The debate we have witnessed in this book demonstrates a good deal of how and where we disagree. All the goodwill in the world does not make infant (paedo) baptism and adult (believers') baptism right at one and the same time. This seems logically impossible, and no amount of work can easily make this difference vanish. What shall we do?

Because of the significance of our differences, at least at this point in church history, we can establish congregations that have differing practices of baptism. If we do not take this approach, we will undoubtedly be left with two practical options: (1) seek to force compliance of individual conscience where there is still profound disagreement, or (2) pursue a downplaying of the importance of Christ's command that only harms the church in the greater sense of fidelity to Christ in the gospel. The first choice violates the hard-won liberty of soul that is now part and parcel of the gains made over the last few centuries by means of evangelical influence in the West. The second choice is the one more often exercised by evangelicals in our day, especially if they put a priority on larger numbers of people and less and less emphasis on faithfulness to "everything [Christ has] commanded" (Matt. 28:19–20). This second path tends to treat all doctrinal differences as unimportant and will logically make all the hard sayings in the Bible smooth and easy, a dangerous course for any Christian church to pursue. For this reason, I am hopeful that this book will seriously challenge this kind of response to baptismal differences.

Finally, we must not miss the fact that, though we are not presently united in our views of baptism, we are united in the gospel of grace. Baptism is important, but it is not the most important thing. Even though we disagree, we can and should find common ground, wherever possible, in the one to whom baptism points us—our Lord Jesus Christ.

Conclusion: Finding Common Ground Amid Disagreement and Agreement

1. George R. Beasley-Murray, *Baptism in the New Testament* (Grand Rapids: Eerdmans, 1973), 295–96.

APPENDIX 1:
ALL INSTANCES OF THE WORDS
FOR BAPTISM IN THE NEW TESTAMENT

BAPTŌ ("DIP," "DIPPED," "DIPPING")

So he called to him, "Father Abraham, have pity on me and send Lazarus to dip the tip of his finger in water and cool my tongue, because I am in agony in this fire."

Luke 16:24

Jesus answered, "It is the one to whom I will give this piece of bread when I have dipped it in the dish." Then, dipping the piece of bread, he gave it to Judas Iscariot, son of Simon.

John 13:26 (twice)

He is dressed in a robe dipped in blood, and his name is the Word of God.

Revelation 19:13

BAPTISTĒS ("BAPTIST")

In those days John the Baptist came, preaching in the Desert of Judea.

Matthew 3:1

"I tell you the truth: Among those born of women there has not risen anyone greater than John the Baptist; yet he who is least in the kingdom of heaven is greater than he."

Matthew 11:11

"From the days of John the Baptist until now, the kingdom of heaven has been forcefully advancing, and forceful men lay hold of it."

Matthew 11:12

[Herod] said to his attendants, "This is John the Baptist; he has risen from the dead! That is why miraculous powers are at work in him."

Matthew 14:2

Prompted by her mother, she said, "Give me here on a platter the head of John the Baptist."   *Matthew 14:8*

[Jesus' disciples] replied, "Some say John the Baptist; others say Elijah; and still others, Jeremiah or one of the prophets."   *Matthew 16:14*

Then the disciples understood that [Jesus] was talking to them about John the Baptist.   *Matthew 17:13*

At once the girl hurried in to the king with the request: "I want you to give me right now the head of John the Baptist on a platter."   *Mark 6:25*

[Jesus' disciples] replied, "Some say John the Baptist; others say Elijah; and still others, one of the prophets."   *Mark 8:28*

When the men came to Jesus, they said, "John the Baptist sent us to you to ask, 'Are you the one who was to come, or should we expect someone else?'"   *Luke 7:20*

"For John the Baptist came neither eating bread nor drinking wine, and you say, 'He has a demon!'"   *Luke 7:33*

[Jesus' disciples] replied, "Some say John the Baptist; others say Elijah; and still others, that one of the prophets of long ago has come back to life."   *Luke 9:19*

BAPTISMA
("BAPTISM," "BAPTIZED," "BAPTIZING")

But when he saw many of the Pharisees and Sadducees coming to where he was baptizing, he said to them: "You brood of vipers! Who warned you to flee from the coming wrath?"   *Matthew 3:7*

"John's baptism—where did it come from? Was it from heaven, or from men?"
         They discussed it among themselves and said, "If we say, 'From heaven,' he will ask, 'Then why didn't you believe him?'"   *Matthew 21:25*

And so John came, baptizing in the desert region and preaching a baptism of repentance for the forgiveness of sins.   *Mark 1:4*

"You don't know what you are asking," Jesus said. "Can you drink the cup I drink or be baptized with the baptism I am baptized with?"   *Mark 10:38*

"We can," [James and John] answered. Jesus said to them, "You will drink the cup I drink and be baptized with the baptism I am baptized with."   *Mark 10:39*

"John's baptism—was it from heaven, or from men? Tell me!"   *Mark 11:30*

[John] went into all the country around the Jordan, preaching a baptism of repentance for the forgiveness of sins.   *Luke 3:3*

"But I [Jesus] have a baptism to undergo, and how distressed I am until it is completed!"   *Luke 12:50*

"John's baptism—was it from heaven, or from men?"
                                                                    Luke 20:4

"beginning from John's baptism to the time when Jesus was taken up from us. For one of these must become a witness with us of his resurrection."   *Acts 1:22*

"You know what has happened throughout Judea, beginning in Galilee after the baptism that John preached—"
                                                                  Acts 10:37

"Before the coming of Jesus, John preached repentance and baptism to all the people of Israel."   *Acts 13:24*

[Apollos] had been instructed in the way of the Lord, and he spoke with great fervor and taught about Jesus accurately, though he knew only the baptism of John.
                                                                  Acts 18:25

So Paul asked, "Then what baptism did you receive?"
     "John's baptism," [the Ephesian disciples] replied.
                                                                    Acts 19:3

Paul said, "John's baptism was a baptism of repentance. He told the people to believe in the one coming after him, that is, in Jesus."   *Acts 19:4*

We were therefore buried with him through baptism into death in order that, just as Christ was raised from the dead through the glory of the Father, we too may live a new life. *Romans 6:4*

one Lord, one faith, one baptism; *Ephesians 4:5*

and this water symbolizes baptism that now saves you also—not the removal of dirt from the body but the pledge of a good conscience toward God. It saves you by the resurrection of Jesus Christ, *1 Peter 3:21*

BAPTISMOS ("BAPTISM," "BAPTISMS," "CEREMONIAL WASHINGS," "WASHING")

When they come from the marketplace they do not eat unless they wash. And they observe many other traditions, such as the washing of cups, pitchers and kettles. *Mark 7:4*

having been buried with him in baptism and raised with him through your faith in the power of God, who raised him from the dead. *Colossians 2:12*

instruction about baptisms, the laying on of hands, the resurrection of the dead, and eternal judgment. *Hebrews 6:2*

They are only a matter of food and drink and various ceremonial washings—external regulations applying until the time of the new order. *Hebrews 9:10*

BAPTIZŌ ("BAPTIZED," "BAPTIZE," "BAPTIZING," "BAPTIST," "WASH," "BAPTISM")

Confessing their sins, [the people] were baptized by [John] in the Jordan River. *Matthew 3:6*

"I [John] baptize you with water for repentance. But after me will come one who is more powerful than I, whose sandals I am not fit to carry. He will baptize you with the Holy Spirit and with fire." *Matthew 3:11*

Then Jesus came from Galilee to the Jordan to be baptized by John. *Matthew 3:13*

But John tried to deter [Jesus], saying, "I need to be baptized by you, and do you come to me?" *Matthew 3:14*

As soon as Jesus was baptized, he went up out of the water. At that moment heaven was opened, and he saw the Spirit of God descending like a dove and lighting on him. *Matthew 3:16*

"Therefore go and make disciples of all nations, baptizing them in the name of the Father and of the Son and of the Holy Spirit, *Matthew 28:19*

And so John came, baptizing in the desert region and preaching a baptism of repentance for the forgiveness of sins. *Mark 1:4*

The whole Judean countryside and all the people of Jerusalem went out to [John]. Confessing their sins, they were baptized by him in the Jordan River. *Mark 1:5*

"I [John] baptize you with water, but [Jesus] will baptize you with the Holy Spirit." *Mark 1:8 (twice)*

At that time Jesus came from Nazareth in Galilee and was baptized by John in the Jordan. *Mark 1:9*

King Herod heard about this, for Jesus' name had become well known. Some were saying, "John the Baptist has been raised from the dead, and that is why miraculous powers are at work in him." *Mark 6:14*

She went out and said to her mother, "What shall I ask for?"
　　"The head of John the Baptist," she answered. *Mark 6:24*

When they come from the marketplace they do not eat unless they wash. And they observe many other traditions, such as the washing of cups, pitchers and kettles. *Mark 7:4*

"You don't know what you are asking," Jesus said. "Can you drink the cup I drink or be baptized with the baptism I am baptized with?" *Mark 10:38 (twice)*

"We can," they answered.
　　Jesus said to them, "You will drink the cup I drink and be baptized with the baptism I am baptized with." *Mark 10:39 (twice)*

"Whoever believes and is baptized will be saved, but whoever does not believe will be condemned."

Mark 16:16

John said to the crowds coming out to be baptized by him, "You brood of vipers! Who warned you to flee from the coming wrath?"

Luke 3:7

Tax collectors also came to be baptized. "Teacher," they asked, "what should we do?"

Luke 3:12

John answered them all, "I baptize you with water. But one more powerful than I will come, the thongs of whose sandals I am not worthy to untie. He will baptize you with the Holy Spirit and with fire."

Luke 3:16 (twice)

When all the people were being baptized, Jesus was baptized too. And as he was praying, heaven was opened.

Luke 3:21 (twice)

All the people, even the tax collectors, when they heard Jesus' words, acknowledged that God's way was right, because they had been baptized by John.

Luke 7:29

But the Pharisees and experts in the law rejected God's purpose for themselves, because they had not been baptized by John.

Luke 7:30

But the Pharisee, noticing that Jesus did not first wash before the meal, was surprised.

Luke 11:38

[Some Pharisees] questioned him, "Why then do you baptize if you are not the Christ, nor Elijah, nor the Prophet?"

John 1:25

"I baptize with water," John replied, "but among you stands one you do not know."

John 1:26

This all happened at Bethany on the other side of the Jordan, where John was baptizing.

John 1:28

"I [John] myself did not know him, but the reason I came baptizing with water was that he might be revealed to Israel."

John 1:31

"I [John] would not have known him, except that the one who sent me to baptize with water told me, 'The man on whom you see the Spirit come down and remain is he who will baptize with the Holy Spirit.'"   *John 1:33 (twice)*

After this, Jesus and his disciples went out into the Judean countryside, where he spent some time with them, and baptized. *John 3:22*

Now John also was baptizing in Aenon near Salim, because there was plenty of water, and people were constantly coming to be baptized. *John 3:23*

[John's disciples] came to John and said to him, "Rabbi, that man who was with you on the other side of the Jordan—the one you testified about—well, he is baptizing, and everyone is going to him." *John 3:26*

The Pharisees heard that Jesus was gaining and baptizing more disciples than John, *John 4:1*

although in fact it was not Jesus who baptized, but his disciples. *John 4:2*

Then Jesus went back across the Jordan to the place where John had been baptizing in the early days. Here he stayed. *John 10:40*

"For John baptized with water, but in a few days you will be baptized with the Holy Spirit." *Acts 1:5 (twice)*

Peter replied, "Repent and be baptized, every one of you, in the name of Jesus Christ for the forgiveness of your sins. And you will receive the gift of the Holy Spirit." *Acts 2:38*

Those who accepted his message were baptized, and about three thousand were added to their number that day. *Acts 2:41*

But when they believed Philip as he preached the good news of the kingdom of God and the name of Jesus Christ, they were baptized, both men and women. *Acts 8:12*

Simon himself believed and was baptized. And he followed Philip everywhere, astonished by the great signs and miracles he saw. *Acts 8:13*

because the Holy Spirit had not yet come upon any of them; they had simply been baptized into the name of the Lord Jesus. *Acts 8:16*

As they traveled along the road, they came to some water and the eunuch said, "Look, here is water. Why shouldn't I be baptized?"   *Acts 8:36*

And he gave orders to stop the chariot. Then both Philip and the eunuch went down into the water and Philip baptized him.   *Acts 8:38*

Immediately, something like scales fell from Saul's eyes, and he could see again. He got up and was baptized.
                                                    Acts 9:18

"Can anyone keep these people from being baptized with water? They have received the Holy Spirit just as we have."   *Acts 10:47*

So he ordered that they be baptized in the name of Jesus Christ. Then they asked Peter to stay with them for a few days.   *Acts 10:48*

"Then I remembered what the Lord had said: 'John baptized with water, but you will be baptized with the Holy Spirit.'"   *Acts 11:16 (twice)*

When [Lydia] and the members of her household were baptized, she invited us to her home. "If you consider me a believer in the Lord," she said, "come and stay at my house." And she persuaded us.   *Acts 16:15*

At that hour of the night the jailer took [Paul and Silas] and washed their wounds; then immediately he and all his family were baptized.   *Acts 16:33*

Crispus, the synagogue ruler, and his entire household believed in the Lord; and many of the Corinthians who heard him believed and were baptized.   *Acts 18:8*

On hearing this, [the Ephesian disciples] were baptized into the name of the Lord Jesus.   *Acts 19:5*

"And now [Saul] what are you waiting for? Get up, be baptized and wash your sins away, calling on [Jesus'] name."   *Acts 22:16*

Or don't you know that all of us who were baptized into Christ Jesus were baptized into his death?
                                          Romans 6:3 (twice)

Is Christ divided? Was Paul crucified for you? Were you baptized into the name of Paul?   *1 Corinthians 1:13*

I am thankful that I did not baptize any of you except Crispus and Gaius.   *1 Corinthians 1:14*

so no one can say that you were baptized into my name.
        1 Corinthians 1:15

(Yes, I also baptized the household of Stephanas; beyond that, I don't remember if I baptized anyone else.)
        1 Corinthians 1:16 (twice)

For Christ did not send me to baptize, but to preach the gospel—not with words of human wisdom, lest the cross of Christ be emptied of its power.   *1 Corinthians 1:17*

They were all baptized into Moses in the cloud and in the sea.   *1 Corinthians 10:2*

For we were all baptized by one Spirit into one body—whether Jews or Greeks, slave or free—and we were all given the one Spirit to drink.
        1 Corinthians 12:13

Now if there is no resurrection, what will those do who are baptized for the dead? If the dead are not raised at all, why are people baptized for them?
        1 Corinthians 15:29 (twice)

For all of you who were baptized into Christ have clothed yourselves with Christ.   *Galatians 3:27*

APPENDIX 2:
STATEMENTS ON BAPTISM
IN CREEDS, CONFESSIONS,
AND CATECHISMS

THE *DIDACHE*

Concerning baptism, thus shall ye baptize. Having first recited all these things, baptize in the name of the Father and of the Son and of the Holy Spirit.

THE NICENE-CONSTANTINOPOLITAN CREED (AD 381)

We believe in one holy catholic and apostolic church. We acknowledge one baptism for the forgiveness of sins. We look for the resurrection of the dead, and the life of the world to come. Amen.

THE AUGSBURG CONFESSION (1530; LUTHERAN)

Article IX

It is taught among us that baptism is necessary and that grace is offered through it. Children, too, should be baptized, for in baptism they are committed to God and become acceptable to him.

On this account the Anabaptists who teach that infant baptism is not right are rejected.

LUTHER'S SMALL CATECHISM (1529)

Part IV: The Sacrament of Holy Baptism

Q. What is baptism?

A. Baptism is not simply common water, but it is the water comprehended in God's command, and connected with God's Word.

Q. What is that Word of God?

A. It is that which our Lord Christ speaks in the last chapter of Matthew [28:19].

Q. What does baptism give, or of what use is it?

A. It works forgiveness of sins, delivers from death and the devil, and gives everlasting salvation to all who believe, as the Word and promise of God declare.

Q. Where are such words and promises of God?

A. Those which our Lord Christ speaks in the last chapter of Mark: "He that believeth and is baptized, shall be saved; but he that believeth not, shall be damned."

Q. How can water do such things?

A. It is not water, indeed, that does it, but the Word of God which is with and in the water, and faith, which trusts in the Word of God in the water. For without the Word of God the water is nothing but water, and no baptism; but with the Word of God it is a baptism — that is, a gracious water of life and a washing of regeneration in the Holy Ghost, as St. Paul says, Titus, third chapter [3:5–7].

Q. What does such baptizing with water signify?

A. It signifies that the old Adam in us is to be drowned by daily sorrow and repentance, and perish with all sins and evil lusts; and that the new man should daily come forth again and rise, who shall live before God in righteousness and purity forever.

Q. Where is it so written?

A. St. Paul in the 6th chapter of Romans says, "We are buried with Christ by baptism into death; that like as he was raised up from the dead by the glory of the Father, even so we also should walk in newness of life."

THE FRENCH CONFESSION OF FAITH (1559; PREPARED BY JOHN CALVIN)

Article XXXV

We confess only two sacraments common to the whole church, of which the first, baptism, is given as a pledge of our adoption; for by it we are grafted into the body of Christ, so as to be washed and cleansed by his blood, and then renewed in purity of life by his Holy Spirit. We hold, also, that although we are baptized only once, yet the gain that it symbolizes to us reaches over our whole lives and to our death, so that we have a lasting witness that Jesus Christ will always be our justification and sanctification. Nevertheless, although it is a sacrament of faith and penitence, yet as God receives little children into the church with their fathers, we say, upon the authority of Jesus Christ, that the children of believing parents should be baptized.

THE BELGIC CONFESSION (1561; REFORMED)

Article XXXIV: Holy Baptism

We believe and confess that Jesus Christ, who is the end of the law, has made an end, by the shedding of his blood, of all other sheddings of blood which men could or would make as a propitiation or satisfaction for sin; and that he, having abolished circumcision, which was done with blood, has instituted the sacrament of baptism instead thereof, by which we are received into the church of God, and separated from all other people and strange religions, that we may wholly belong to him whose ensign and banner we bear, and which serves as a testimony unto us that he will forever be our gracious God and father.

Therefore he has commanded all those who are his to be baptized with pure water, into the name of the Father and of the Son and of the Holy Spirit: thereby signifying to us, that as water washes away the filth of the body when poured upon it, and is seen on the body of the baptized when sprinkled upon him, so does the blood of Christ, by the power of the Holy Spirit, internally sprinkle the soul, cleanse it from its sins, and regenerate us from children of wrath unto children of God. Not that this is effected by the external water, but by the sprinkling of the precious blood of the Son of God; who is our Red Sea, through which we must pass to escape the tyranny of Pharaoh, that is, the devil, and to enter into the spiritual land of Canaan.

Therefore, the ministers, on their part, administer the sacrament and that which is visible, but our Lord gives that which is signified by the sacrament, namely, the gifts and invisible grace; washing, cleansing, and purging our souls of all filth and unrighteousness; renewing our hearts and filling them with all comfort; giving unto us a true assurance of his fatherly goodness; putting on us the new man, and putting off the old man with all his deeds.

Therefore, we believe that every man who is earnestly studious of obtaining life eternal ought to be but once baptized with this only baptism, without ever repeating the same, since we can not be born twice. Neither does this baptism avail us only at the time when the water is poured upon us and received by us, but also through the whole course of our life.

Therefore we detest the error of the Anabaptists, who are not content with the one only baptism they have once received, and moreover condemn the baptism of the infants of believers, who, we believe ought to be baptized and sealed with the sign of the covenant, as the children in Israel formerly were circumcised upon the same promises which are made unto our children. And indeed Christ shed his blood no less for the washing of the children of the faithful than for adult persons; and therefore they ought to receive the sign and sacrament of that which Christ has done for them; as the Lord commanded in the law that they should be made partakers of the sacrament of Christ's suffering and death shortly after they were born, by offering for them a lamb, which was a sacrament of Jesus Christ. Moreover, what circumcision was to the Jews, baptism is to our children. And for this reason Paul calls baptism the circumcision of Christ.

THE SECOND HELVETIC CONFESSION OF FAITH (1566; REFORMED; PREPARED BY HEINRICH BULLINGER)

Chapter XIX: Of the Sacraments of the Church of Christ

But the principal thing which God promises in all sacraments and to which all the godly in all ages direct their attention (some call it the substance and matter of sacraments) is Christ the Savior—that only sacrifice (Heb. 10:12), and that Lamb of God slain from the foundation of the world (Rev. 13:8); that rock, also, from which all our fathers drank (1 Cor. 10:4), by whom all the elect are circumcised without hands through the Holy Spirit (Col. 2:11–12), and are washed from all their sins (Rev. 1:5), and are nourished with the very body and blood of Christ unto eternal life (John 6:54).

Chapter XX: Of Holy Baptism

Baptism was instituted and consecrated by God; and the first that baptized was John, who dipped Christ in the water in Jordan. From him it came to the apostles, who also baptized with water. The Lord expressly commanded them to preach the Gospel and to baptize "in the name of the Father and of the Son and of the Holy Spirit" (Matt. 28:19). And in Acts, Peter said to the Jews who inquired what they ought to do: "Be baptized, every one of you, in the name of Jesus Christ for the forgiveness of your sins; and you shall receive the gift of the Holy Spirit" (Acts 2:38). Hence baptism is called by some a sign of initiation for God's people, since by it the elect of God are consecrated unto God.

There is but one baptism in the Church of God; and it is sufficient to be once baptized or consecrated unto God. For baptism once received continues for all of life, and is a perpetual sealing of our adoption.

Now to be baptized in the name of Christ is to be enrolled, entered, and received into the covenant and family, and so into the inheritance of the sons of God; yes, and in this life to be called after the name of God; that is to say, to be called a son of God; to be purged also from the filthiness of sins, and to be granted the manifold grace of God, in order to lead a new and innocent life. Baptism, therefore, calls to mind and renews the great benefit of God performed to mankind. For we are all born into pollution of sin and are the children of wrath. But God, who is rich in mercy, freely purges us from our sins by the blood of his Son, and in him adopts us to be his sons, and by a holy covenant joins us to himself, and enriches us with various gifts, that we might live a new life. All these things are sealed up unto us in baptism. For inwardly we are regenerated, purified, and renewed by God through the Holy Spirit; and outwardly we receive the sealing of most notable gifts by the water, by which also those great benefits are represented, and, as it were, set before our eyes to be looked upon.

And therefore are we baptized, that is, washed or sprinkled with visible water. For the water makes clean that which is filthy, and refreshes and cools the bodies that fail or faint. And the grace of God deals in like manner with the soul; and does so invisibly and spiritually.

Moreover, by the sacrament of baptism God separates us from all other religions and nations, and consecrates us a peculiar people to himself. We, therefore, by being baptized, confess our faith and are bound to give unto God obedience, mortification of the flesh, and newness of life; yes, and we are soldiers enlisted for the holy warfare of Christ, that all our life long we should fight against the world, Satan, and our own flesh. Moreover, we are baptized into one body of the Church, that we might well agree with all the members of the Church in the one religion and mutual duties.

We believe that the most perfect form of baptism is that by which Christ was baptized, and by which the apostles baptized. Those things, therefore, which by man's device were added afterwards and used in the Church we do not consider necessary to the perfection of baptism. Of this kind is exorcism, the use of lights, oil, spittle, and such other things; as, namely, that baptism is twice every year consecrated with a multitude of ceremonies. But we believe that the baptism of the Church, which is but one, was sanctified in God's first institution of it, and is consecrated by the Word, and is also effectual today in virtue of God's first blessing.

We teach that baptism should not be administered in the Church by women or midwives. For Paul secludes women from ecclesiastical callings; and baptism belongs to ecclesiastical offices.

We condemn the Anabaptists, who deny that young infants, born of faithful parents, are to be baptized. For, according to the doctrine of the Gospel, "theirs is the kingdom of God" (Luke 18:16), and they are written in the covenant of God (Acts 3:25). Why, then, should not the sign of the covenant of God be given to them? Why should they not be consecrated by holy baptism, who are God's peculiar people and are in the Church of God? We condemn also the Anabaptists in the rest of their peculiar opinions which they hold against the Word of God. We therefore are not Anabaptists and have nothing in common with them.

THE WESTMINSTER CONFESSION OF FAITH
(1646; PRESBYTERIAN)

Chapter XXVII: Of the Sacraments

Sacraments are holy signs and seals of the covenant of grace, immediately instituted by God, to represent Christ and his benefits, and to confirm our interest in him: as also to put a visible difference between those that belong unto the Church and the rest of the world; and solemnly to engage them to the service of God in Christ, according to his Word.

There is in every sacrament a spiritual relation or sacramental union between the sign and the thing signified; whence it comes to pass that the names and effects of the one are attributed to the other.

The grace which is exhibited in or by the sacraments, rightly used, is not conferred by any power in them; neither does the efficacy of a sacrament depend upon the piety or intention of him that administers it, but upon the work of the Spirit and the word of institution, which contains, together with a precept authorizing the use thereof, a promise of benefit to worthy receivers.

There are only two sacraments ordained by Christ our Lord in the gospel, that is to say, Baptism and the Supper of the Lord: neither of which may be dispensed by any but by a minister of the Word lawfully ordained.

The sacraments of the Old Testament, in regard of the spiritual things thereby signified and exhibited, were, for substance, the same with those of the New.

Chapter XXVIII: Of Baptism

Baptism is a sacrament of the New Testament, ordained by Jesus Christ, not only for the solemn admission of the party baptized into the visible Church, but also to be unto him a sign and seal of the covenant of grace, of his ingrafting into Christ, of regeneration, of remission of sins, and of his giving up unto God through Jesus Christ to walk in newness of life: which sacrament is, by Christ's own appointment, to be continued in his Church until the end of the world.

The outward element to be used in this sacrament is water, wherewith the party is to be baptized in the name of the Father and of the Son and of the Holy Spirit by a minister of the gospel lawfully called thereunto.

Dipping of the person into the water is not necessary; but baptism is rightly administered by pouring or sprinkling water upon the person.

Not only those who do actually profess faith in and obedience unto Christ but also the infants of one or both believing parents are to be baptized.

Although it is a great sin to contemn or neglect this ordinance, yet grace and salvation are not so inseparably annexed unto it, as that no person can be regenerated or saved without it, or that all who are baptized are undoubtedly regenerated.

The efficacy of baptism is not tied to that moment of time wherein it is administered; yet, notwithstanding, by the right use of this ordinance the grace promised is not only offered but really exhibited and conferred by the Holy Spirit to such (whether of age or infants) as that grace belongs unto, according to the counsel of God's own will, in his appointed time.

The sacrament of baptism is but once to be administered to any person.

THE CONFESSION OF THE WALDENSES
(1655; FROM CALVINISTS IN ITALY)

Article XXVIII

That God does not only instruct us by his Word, but has also ordained certain sacraments to be joined with it, as means to unite us to Jesus Christ, and to make us partakers of his benefits; and that there are only two of them belonging in common to all the members of the Church under the New Testament—to wit, baptism and the Lord's Supper.

Article XXIX

That Christ has instituted the sacrament of baptism to be a testimony of our adoption, and that therein we are cleansed from our sins by the blood of Jesus Christ, and renewed in holiness of life.

THE THIRTY-NINE ARTICLES (1563; ANGLICAN)

XXVII: Of Baptism

Baptism is not only a sign of profession, and mark of difference, whereby Christian men are discerned from others that be not christened, but it is also a sign of regeneration or new birth, whereby, as by an instrument, they that receive baptism rightly are grafted into the Church; the promises of the forgiveness of sin, and of our adoption to be the sons of God by the Holy Spirit, are visibly signed and sealed; faith is confirmed, and grace increased by virtue of prayer unto God.

The baptism of young children is in any wise to be retained in the Church, as most agreeable with the institution of Christ.

THE HEIDELBERG CATECHISM
(1563; REFORMED; PREPARED BY
ZACHARIAS URSINUS AND CASPAR OLEVIANUS)

Lord's Day 25

Q. 65. It is by faith alone that we share in Christ and all his blessings: where then does that faith come from?

A. The Holy Spirit produces it in our heart by the preaching of the holy gospel, and confirms it by the use of the holy sacraments.

Q. 66. What are sacraments?

A. Sacraments are holy signs and seals for us to see. They were instituted by God so that by our use of them he might make us understand more clearly the promise of the gospel, and might put his seal on that promise.

And this is God's gospel promise: to forgive our sins and give us eternal life by grace alone because of Christ's one sacrifice finished on the cross.

Q. 67. Are both the word and the sacraments then intended to focus our faith on the sacrifice of Jesus Christ on the cross as the only ground of our salvation?

A. Right!

In the gospel the Holy Spirit teaches us and through the holy sacraments he assures us that our entire salvation rests on Christ's one sacrifice for us on the cross.

Q. 68. How many sacraments did Christ institute in the New Testament?

A. Two: baptism and the Lord's Supper.

Lord's Day 26

Q. 69. How does baptism remind you and assure you that Christ's one sacrifice on the cross is for you personally?

A. In this way: Christ instituted this outward washing and with it gave the promise that, as surely as water washes away the dirt from the body, so certainly his blood and his Spirit wash away my soul's impurity, in other words, all my sins.

Q. 70. What does it mean to be washed with Christ's blood and Spirit?

A. To be washed with Christ's blood means that God, by grace, has forgiven my sins because of Christ's blood poured out for me in his sacrifice on the cross.

To be washed with Christ's Spirit means that the Holy Spirit has renewed me and set me apart to be a member of Christ so that more and more I become dead to sin and increasingly live a holy and blameless life.

Q. 71. Where does Christ promise that we are washed with his blood and Spirit as surely as we are washed with the water of baptism?

A. In the institution of baptism where he says:

"Therefore go and make disciples of all nations, baptizing them in the name of the Father and of the Son and of the Holy Spirit."

"Whoever believes and is baptized will be saved, but whoever does not believe will be condemned."

This promise is repeated when Scripture calls baptism the washing of rebirth and the washing away of sins.

Q. 72. Does this outward washing with water itself wash away sins?

A. No, only Jesus Christ's blood and the Holy Spirit cleanse us from all sins.

Q. 73. Why then does the Holy Spirit call baptism the washing of rebirth and the washing away of sins?

A. God has good reasons for these words. He wants to teach us that the blood and Spirit of Christ wash away our sins just as water washes away dirt from our bodies.

But more important, he wants to assure us, by this divine pledge and sign, that the washing away of our sins spiritually is as real as physical washing with water.

Q. 74. Should infants, too, be baptized?

A. Yes. Infants as well as adults are in God's covenant and are his people. They, no less than adults, are promised the forgiveness of sin through Christ's blood and the Holy Spirit who produces faith.

Therefore, by baptism, the mark of the covenant, infants should be received into the Christian church and should be distinguished from the children of unbelievers. This was done in the Old Testament by circumcision, which was replaced in the New Testament by baptism.

THE DORDRECHT CONFESSION (1632; MENNONITE)

Article VII: Of Holy Baptism

Regarding baptism, we confess that all penitent believers, who through faith, the new birth, and renewal of the Holy Spirit, have become united with God, and whose names are recorded in heaven, must on such Scriptural confession of their faith, and renewal of life, be baptized with water, in the most worthy name of the Father, and of the Son, and of the Holy Spirit, according to the command of Christ, and the teaching, example, and practice of the apostles, to the burying of their sins, and thus be incorporated into the communion of the saints; whereupon they must learn to observe all things whatsoever the Son of God taught, left on record, and commanded his followers to do.

THE FIRST LONDON CONFESSION OF FAITH (1646; BAPTIST)

Article XXXIX

Baptism is an ordinance of the New Testament, given by Christ, to be dispensed upon persons professing faith, or that are made disciples; who upon profession of faith, ought to be baptized, and after to partake of the Lord's Supper.

Article XL

That the way and manner of dispensing this ordinance, is dipping or plunging the body under water; it being a sign, must answer the things signified, which is, that interest the saints have in the death, burial, and resurrection of Christ: And that as certainly as the body is buried under water, and risen again, so certainly shall the bodies of the saints be raised by the power of Christ, in the day of the resurrection, to reign with Christ.

Article XLI

The person designed by Christ to dispense baptism, the Scripture holds forth to be a disciple; it being nowhere tied to a particular church officer, or person extraordinarily sent the commission enjoining the administration, being given to them as considered disciples, being men able to preach the gospel.

THE PHILADELPHIA CONFESSION OF FAITH (1742; BAPTIST)

Chapter XXIX: Of Baptism and the Lord's Supper

Baptism and the Lord's Supper are ordinances of positive and sovereign institution, appointed by the Lord Jesus, the only lawgiver, to be continued in his church to the end of the world.

These holy appointments are to be administered by those only who are qualified and thereunto called, according to the commission of Christ.

Chapter XXX: Of Baptism

Baptism is an ordinance of the New Testament, ordained by Jesus Christ, to be unto the party baptized, a sign of his fellowship with him in his death and resurrection; of his being engrafted into him; of remission of sins; and of his giving up into God, through Jesus Christ, to live and walk in newness of life.

Those who do actually profess repentance towards God, faith in, and obedience to our Lord Jesus, are the only proper subjects of this ordinance.

The outward element to be used in this ordinance is water, wherein the party is to be baptized, in the name of the Father and of the Son and of the Holy Spirit.

Immersion, or dipping of the person in water, is necessary to the due administration of this ordinance.

THE ARTICLES OF RELIGION (1784; METHODIST)

XVI: Of the Sacraments

Sacraments ordained of Christ are not only badges or tokens of Christian men's profession, but rather they are certain signs of grace, and God's goodwill toward us, by the which he works invisibly in us, and not only quickens, but also strengthens and confirms our faith in him.

There are two sacraments ordained of Christ our Lord in the gospel; that is to say, baptism and the Supper of the Lord.

Those five commonly called sacraments, that is to say, confirmation, penance, orders, matrimony, and extreme unction, are not to be counted for sacraments of the gospel, being such as have partly grown out of the corrupt following of the apostles; and partly are states of life allowed in the Scriptures, but yet have not the like nature of baptism and the Lord's Supper, because they have not any visible sign or ceremony ordained of God.

The sacraments were not ordained of Christ to be gazed upon, or to be carried about, but that we should duly use them. And in such only as worthily receive the same they have a wholesome effect or operation; but they that receive them unworthily purchase to themselves condemnation, as St. Paul says, [in] 1 Corinthians 11:29.

XVII: Of Baptism

Baptism is not only a sign of profession, and mark of difference, whereby Christians are distinguished from others that are not baptized; but it is also a sign of regeneration, or the new birth. The baptism of young children is to be retained in the Church.

CONFESSION OF THE EVANGELICAL
FREE CHURCH OF GENEVA (1848)

Article XVI

We believe that the Savior has instituted baptism and the Lord's Supper as symbols and pledges of the salvation which he has acquired for us: baptism, which is the sign of the purification by the blood and spirit of Jesus Christ; the Eucharist, in which we receive by faith his body and blood, and announce his death until his coming.

APPENDIX 3:
QUOTATIONS ON BAPTISM

QUOTATIONS FROM MARTIN LUTHER ON BAPTISM

Luther's Small Catechism

Baptism signifies that the old Adam in us is to be drowned by daily sorrow and repentance, and perish with all sins and evil lusts; and that the new man should daily come forth again and rise, who shall live before God in righteousness and purity forever.

It is not the water that produces these effects, but the Word of God connected with the water, and our faith which relies on the Word of God connected with the water. For without the Word of God the water is merely water and no baptism.

Luther's Large Catechism

We are not to regard [baptism] as an indifferent matter, then, like putting on a new red coat. It is of the greatest importance that we regard baptism as excellent, glorious, and exalted. It is the chief cause of our contentions and battles because the world now is full of sects who proclaim that baptism is an external thing and that external things are of no use. But no matter how external it may be, here stand God's Word and command which have instituted, established, and confirmed baptism. What God institutes and commands cannot be useless. It is a most precious thing, even though to all appearances it may not be worth a straw.

To be baptized in God's name is to be baptized not by men but by God himself. Although it is performed by men's hands, it is nevertheless truly God's act. From this fact everyone can easily conclude that it is of much greater value than the work of any man or saint. For what work can man do that is greater than God's work?

[Baptism] is nothing else than divine water, not that the water in itself is nobler than other water but that God's Word and commandment are added to it.

Note this distinction then: baptism is a very different thing from all other water, not by virtue of the natural substance but because here something nobler is added. God himself stakes his honor, his power, and his might on it. Therefore it is not simply a natural water, but a divine, heavenly, holy, and blessed water—praise it in any other terms you can—all by virtue of the Word, which is a heavenly, holy Word which no one can sufficiently extol, for it contains and conveys all the fullness of God. From the Word it derives its nature as a sacrament, as St. Augustine taught: "*Aocedat verbum ad elementum et fit sacramentum.*" This means that when the Word is added to the element or the natural substance, it becomes a sacrament, that is, a holy, divine thing and sign.

I therefore admonish you again that these two, the Word and the water, must by no means be separated from each other. For where the Word is separated from the water, the water is no different from that which the maid cooks with and could indeed be called a bathkeeper's baptism. But when the Word is present according to God's ordinance, baptism is a sacrament, and it is called Christ's baptism. This is the first point to be emphasized: the nature and dignity of this holy sacrament.

Since we have learned the great benefit and power of baptism, let us observe further who receives these gifts and benefits of baptism. This again is most beautifully and clearly expressed in these same words, "He who believes and is baptized shall be saved," that is, faith alone makes the person worthy to receive the salutary divine water profitably. Since these blessings are offered and promised in the word which accompany the water, they cannot be received unless we believe them whole-heartedly. Without faith baptism is of no use, although in itself it is an infinite divine treasure.

Thus you plainly see that baptism is not a work which we do but is a treasure which God gives and faith grasps, just as the Lord Christ upon the cross is not a work but a treasure comprehended and offered to us in the Word and received by faith.

QUOTATIONS FROM JOHN CALVIN ON BAPTISM

Calvin's Commentaries

Whoever, having neglected baptism, feigns himself to be contented with the bare promise, tramples as much as in him lies, upon the blood of Christ, or at least does not suffer it to flow for the washing of his own children. Therefore just punishment follows the contempt of the sign, in the privation of grace; because ... the covenant of God is violated (Commentary on Genesis, 1:458).

Baptism [is] a pledge of eternal life before God ... an outward sign of faith before men (Commentary on the Synoptic Gospels, 3:385).

Everyone profits so much in baptism as he learns to look unto Christ.... The whole strength of baptism is contained in Christ (Commentary on Acts, 1:120).

Baptism, viewed in regard to us, is a passive work: we bring nothing to it but faith; and all that belongs to it is laid up in Christ (Commentary on Galatians, 150).

Institutes of the Christian Religion

Now baptism was given to us by God for these ends (which I have taught to be common to all sacraments): first, to serve our faith before him; secondly, to serve our confession before men (4:15:1).

But we must realize that at whatever time we are baptized, we are once for all washed and purged for our whole life. Therefore, as often as we fall away, we ought to recall the memory of our baptism and fortify our mind with it, that we may always be sure and confident of the forgiveness of sins (4:15:3).

Lastly, our faith receives from baptism the advantage of its sure testimony to us that we are not only engrafted into the death and life of Christ, but so united to Christ himself that we become sharers in all his blessings (4:15:6).

But whether the person being baptized should be wholly immersed, and whether thrice or once, whether he should only be sprinkled with poured water — these details are of no importance, but ought to be optional to churches according to the diversity of countries. Yet the word "baptize" means to immerse, and it is clear that the rite of immersion was observed in the ancient church (4:15:19).

Few realize how much injury the dogma that baptism is necessary for salvation, badly expounded, has entailed. As a consequence, they are less cautious. For, where the opinion has prevailed that all are lost who have not happened to be baptized with water, our condition is worse than that of God's ancient people — as if the grace of God were now more restricted than under the law! (4:15:20).

But this principle will easily and immediately settle the controversy: infants are not barred from the Kingdom of Heaven just because they happen to depart the present life before they have been immersed in water. Yet we have already seen that serious injustice is done to God's covenant if we do not assent to it, as if it were weak of itself, since its effect depends neither upon baptism nor upon any additions (4:15:22).

If it is right for infants to be brought to Christ, why not also to be received into baptism, the symbol of our communion and fellowship with Christ? If the Kingdom of Heaven belongs to them, why is the sign denied which, so to speak, opens to them a door into the church, that, adopted into it, they may be enrolled among the heirs of the Kingdom of Heaven? How unjust of us to drive away those whom Christ calls to himself! (4:16:7).

Tracts and Letters

The salvation of infants is included in the promise in which God declares to believers that he will be a God to them and to their seed.... Their salvation, therefore, has not its commencement in baptism, but being already founded on the word, is sealed by baptism (3:109–10, Antidote to the Council of Trent).

Those who were baptized when mere infants, God regenerates in childhood or adolescence, occasionally even in old age (Tracts 2:218, Mutual Consent in Regard to the Sacraments).

QUOTATIONS FROM JOHN WESLEY ON BAPTISM (FROM *JOHN WESLEY ON CHRISTIAN BELIEFS*, KENNETH CAIN KINGHORN, ED. [NASHVILLE: ABINGDON, 2002])

The new birth is represented by baptism, which is the beginning of a complete restoration to life (p. 63).

The new birth is not baptism. The two are not the same thing. To be sure, many people seem to imagine that both are essentially alike. At least they speak as if they think the two are identical. Yet, I do not know that this belief is publicly professed by any Christian denomination at all. Certainly no church within the British Empire holds this view — not the established Church or any of the dissenting churches (p. 235).

What can be more obvious than that the application of water is an external work, and the coming of the Holy Spirit is an internal work? It is clear that the one is a visible thing and the other is an invisible thing. The two are entirely distinct from each other. One is a human act that washes the body, and the other is an act of God done in the soul. The rite of baptism is just as separable from regeneration as the body is from the soul, or water is from the Holy Spirit (p. 236).

Do not say in your heart, "I was once baptized, so therefore I am now a child of God." I truly regret that the work done in your baptism will by no means automatically continue throughout your life. How many baptized gluttons, drunkards, liars and common swearers, abusive critics, and gossips, whoremongers, thieves, extortioners are there? What do you think? Are these people now the children of God? Indeed, whoever you are, if you are one of these people I say to you, "You are from your father the devil, and you choose to do your father's desires." In the name of him whom you crucify afresh, I call out to you. In the very words that Jesus spoke to your circumcised predecessors, I declare, "You snakes, you brood of vipers! How can you escape being sentenced to hell?" (p. 309).

All of you who do not have these marks of the new birth on your souls (whether you were baptized or are unbaptized) need to receive these marks in your lives. Without them, you will certainly perish everlastingly (p. 310).

QUOTATIONS FROM CHARLES H. SPURGEON ON BAPTISM

The New Park Street Pulpit

I should think it a high sin and treason against heaven, if, believing that baptism signifies immersion, and immersion only, I should pretend to administer it by sprinkling; or, believing that baptism appertains to believers only, I should consider myself a criminal in the sight of God if I should give it to any but those who believe (4:170).

The Metropolitan Tabernacle Pulpit

I do not question the safety of the soul that has believed, but I do say again, I would not run the risk of the man who, having believed, refuses to be baptized (16:156).

As long as you give baptism to an unregenerate child, people will imagine that it must do the child good; for they will ask, If it does not do it any good, why is it baptized? (19:556).

Do not make any mistake, and imagine that immersion in water can wash away sin; but do remember that if the

Lord puts this outward profession side by side with the washing away of sins it is not a trifling matter (31:251).

I feel shocked when I hear people say, "But it is not essential to salvation." You mean and beggarly spirit! Will you do nothing but what is essential to your own salvation? A Pharisee or a harlot might talk so. Is this your love to Christ—that you will not obey him, unless he shall pay you for it, unless he shall make your soul's salvation depend upon it? (36:56).

Several sects claim apostolic succession, and if any possess it, the Baptists are the most likely, since they practice the ordinances as they were delivered; but we do not even care to trace our pedigree through the long line of martyrs, and of men abhorred by ecclesiastics. If we could do this without a break, the result would be of no value in our eyes; for the rag of "apostolic succession" is not worth warehouse-room. Those who contend for the fiction may monopolize it if they will (37:40).

I am amazed that an unconscious babe should be made the partaker of an ordinance which, according to the plain teaching of the Scriptures, requires the conscious acquiescence and complete heart-trust of the recipient. Very few, if any, would argue that infants ought to receive the Lord's Supper; but there is no more Scriptural warrant for bringing them to the one ordinance than there is for bringing them to the other (47:351).

QUOTATIONS FROM CHURCH FATHERS ON BAPTISM

Augustine

(He) who has been baptized in the Church, should he become a deserter from the Church, will lack holiness but will not lack the seal of the sacrament.... Just as the man who is a deserter from the army loses legal status without losing his citizenship.

In so far as I can judge, it is already as clear as crystal that in this question of baptism what is to be considered is not who confers but what is conferred; not who receives but what is received; not who has it but what he has.

Basil the Great

For prisoners, baptism is ransom, forgiveness of debts, death of sin, regeneration of the soul, a resplendent garment, an unbreakable seal, a chariot to heaven, a protector royal, a gift of adoption.

Let no one be misled by the fact that the Apostle frequently omits the name of the Father and of the Holy Spirit when mentioning baptism; nor let anyone suppose that the invocation of the Names is a matter of indifference. "Those of you," he says, "who have been baptized in Christ have put on Christ," and again, "Those of you who have been baptized in Christ have been baptized in his death." The naming of Christ, you see, is the confession of the whole; it bespeaks the God who anoints, the Son who is anointed, and the Spirit who is the anointing.

This then is what it means to be born again of water and Spirit; just as our dying is effected in the water, our living is wrought through the Spirit. If, therefore, there is any grace in the water, it is not from the nature of water but the Spirit's presence there.

Cyril of Jerusalem

Since man is of twofold nature, composed of body and soul, the purification also is twofold.... The water cleanses the body, and the Spirit seals the soul.

Gregory of Nazianzus

... [T]he virtue of Baptism is to be understood as a covenant with God for a second life.

In whose name were you baptized? In the Father's name? Jewish, but good. In the Son's name? Good; no longer Jewish, but not yet perfect. In the Holy Spirit's name? Excellent! This is perfect.

John Chrysostom

Lest through a confidence in the gift of the font you should turn negligent of your conversation [way of life] after it, even supposing you receive baptism, yet if you are not minded to be led by the Spirit afterwards, you lose the dignity bestowed upon you and the pre-eminence of your adoption.

Justin Martyr

This is how we dedicate ourselves to God after being newly created through Christ. We bring them to somewhere where there is water, for they then wash themselves in the water in the name of God the Father and Lord of all, and of our Savior Jesus Christ and of the Holy Spirit.

Origen

Not everyone who is washed receives salvation. We who have received the grace of baptism in the name of Christ have been washed; but I do not know which of us has been washed to salvation.

Tertullian

Those who are going to be baptized must pray repeatedly, fasting and kneeling and in vigils, and confess all their past sins.

OTHER CHRISTIANS
ON BAPTISM

James P. Boyce
(nineteenth-century Baptist theologian)

Baptism is an ordinance of the Lord Jesus, obligatory upon every believer, wherein he is immersed in water in the name of the Father and of the Son and of the Holy Spirit, as a sign of his fellowship with the death and resurrection of Christ, of remission of sins, and of his giving himself up to God, to live and walk in newness of life. It is prerequisite to church fellowship and to participation in the Lord's Supper.

Martin Bucer
(sixteenth-century German Reformer)

Our regeneration and our renewal through the Holy Spirit are offered us and showed us, revealed through words and washing in water.

J. Alec Motyer
(twentieth-century Bible expositor)

Baptism points back to the work of God, and forward to the life of faith.

Friedrich Rest
(twentieth-century author)

In baptism, the Christian is born. His old self is buried and the new self emerges. Whether in the case of infants or adults, baptism signifies this more as a promise than as an actually fulfilled fact. The direction is indicated rather than the arrival.

Friedrich Schleiermacher
(nineteenth-century German theologian)

There will always be some regenerate persons who are not yet baptized but who might well have claimed to be received earlier into the Church; similarly there will be baptized persons who are not yet regenerate but in the most active way are being commended to divine grace for regeneration by the prayers of the Church.

Menno Simons
(sixteenth-century Anabaptist leader)

We have not a single command in the Scriptures that infants are baptized, or that the apostles practiced it. Therefore we confess with good sense that infant baptism is nothing but a human invention and notion.

RESOURCES FOR FURTHER STUDY

Adams, Jay E. *The Meaning and Mode of Baptism*. Phillipsburg, N.J.: Presbyterian & Reformed, 1975.

Aland, Kurt. *Did the Early Church Baptize Infants?* London: SCM Press, 1963.

Armour, Rollin S. *Anabaptist Baptism*. Scottdale, Pa.: Herald, 1966.

Baillie, John. *Baptism and Conversion*. New York: Charles Scribner's, 1963.

Barth, Karl. *The Teaching of the Church Regarding Baptism*. London: SCM Press, 1948.

Beasley-Murray, G. R. *Baptism in the New Testament*. Grand Rapids: Eerdmans, 1973.

Booth, Robert R. *Children of the Promise: The Biblical Case for Infant Baptism*. Phillipsburg, N.J.: Presbyterian & Reformed, 1995.

Bridge, Donald, and David Phypers. *The Water That Divides: A Survey of the Doctrine of Baptism*. Fearn, Ross-shire, Scotland: Christian Focus Press, 1998.

Bromiley, G. W. *Baptism and the Anglican Reformers*. Cambridge: Lutterworth, 1953.

———. *Children of Promise: The Case for Baptizing Infants*. Grand Rapids: Eerdmans, 1979.

———. *Sacramental Teaching and Practice in the Reformation Church*. Grand Rapids: Eerdmans, 1957.

———. *The Unity and Disunity of the Church*. Grand Rapids: Eerdmans, 1958.

Brooks, Oscar S. *The Drama of Decision: Baptism in the New Testament*. Peabody, Mass.: Hendrickson, 1987.

Buchanan, Colin. *Baptismal Discipline*. Cambridge: Grove Books, 1972.

———. *A Case for Infant Baptism*. Cambridge: Grove Books, 1973.

Burgess, John R. *After Baptism: Shaping the Christian Life*. Louisville: Westminster, 2005.

Burnish, Raymond F. G. *The Meaning of Baptism*. London: SPCK, 1985.

Carson, Alexander. *Baptism in Its Modes and Subjects*. Philadelphia: American Baptist Publications Society, 1860.

Clark, Neville. *An Approach to the Theology of the Sacraments*. London: SCM Press, 1956.

Cottrell, Jack. *Baptism: A Biblical Study*. Joplin, Mo.: College Press, 1989.

Cullman, Oscar. *Baptism in the New Testament*. London: SCM Press, 1950.

Cully, Kendig Brubaker. *Sacraments: A Language of Faith*. Philadelphia: Christina Education Press, 1961.

Dale, James W. *Christic and Patristic Baptism*. Monmouth, Ill.: Balchazy-Carducci, 1975.

Eller, Vernard. *In Place of Sacraments: A Study of Baptism and the Lord's Supper*. Grand Rapids: Eerdmans, 1972.

Felton, Gayle C. *The Gift of Water: The Practice and Theology of Baptism Among Methodists in America*. Nashville: Abingdon, 1972.

Fiedler, Ernest J., and R. Benjamin Garrison. *The Sacraments: An Experiment in Ecumenical Honesty*. Nashville: Abingdon, 1969.

Fisher, J. D. C. *Christian Initiation: Baptism in the Medieval West*. London: SPCK, 1965.

———. *Christian Initiation: The Reformation Period*. London: SPCK, 1970.

Flemington, W. F. *The New Testament Doctrine of Baptism*. London: SPCK, 1957.

Forsyth, Peter Taylor. *The Church and the Sacraments*. London: Independent Press, 1964.

Gaukroger, Stephen. *Being Baptized*. London: Marshall-Pickering, 1992.

Gilmore, Alec. *Baptism and Christian Unity*. Valley Forge, Pa.: Judson, 1966.

———, ed. *Christian Baptism*. Valley Forge, Pa.: Judson, 1959.

Green, Michael. *Baptism: Its Purpose, Practice and Power*. Downers Grove, Ill.: InterVarsity, 1987.

Guy, Laurie. *Introducing Early Christianity: A Topical Survey of Its Life, Beliefs, and Practices*. Downers Grove, Ill.: InterVarsity, 2004.

Jeremias, Joachim. *Infant Baptism in the First Four Centuries*. London: SCM Press, 1959.

———. *The Origins of Infant Baptism*. London: SCM Press, 1963.

Jewett, Paul K. *Infant Baptism and the Covenant of Grace*. Grand Rapids: Eerdmans, 1978.

Kavanagh, Aidan. *The Shape of Baptism: The Rite of Christian Initiation*. Collegeville, Minn.: Liturgical, 1978.

Kingdon, David. *Children of Abraham*. Sussex, England: Carey Publications, 1973.

Lampe, G. W. H. *The Seal of the Spirit*. London: SPCK, 1967.

Marcel, Pierre C. *The Biblical Doctrine of Infant Baptism*. Edinburgh: James Clarke, 1953.

Marty, Martin. *Baptism*. Minneapolis: Fortress, 1977.

Mauro, Philip. *Baptism: Its Place and Importance in Christianity*. London: Morgan & Scott, 1914.

Murray, John. *Christian Baptism*. Phillipsburg, N.J.: Presbyterian & Reformed, 1962.

Osborne, Kenan B. *The Christian Sacraments of Initiation*. Mahwah, N.J.: Paulist, 1987.

Pawson, David, and Colin Buchanan. *Infant Baptism Under Cross-Examination*. Cambridge: Grove Books, 1974.

Rahner, Karl. *The Church and the Sacraments*. New York: Hyperion, 1994.

———. *Holy Baptism*. Minneapolis: Dimension, 1989.

Riggs, John W. *Baptism in the Reformed Tradition: An Historical and Practical Theology*. Louisville: Westminster, 2002.

Riley, Hugh. *Christian Initiation: A Comparative Study of the Interpretation of the Baptismal Liturgy*. Washington, D.C.: Catholic University of America Press, 1974.

Root, Michael, and Risto Saarinen, eds. *Baptism and the Unity of the Church*. Grand Rapids: Eerdmans, 1998.

Roy, Kevin. *Baptism, Reconciliation and Unity*. Carlisle, Cumbria, England: Paternoster, 1997.

Sartelle, John P. *Infant Baptism*. Phillipsburg, N.J.: Presbyterian & Reformed, 1985.

Schenck, Lewis Bevins. *The Presbyterian Doctrine of Children in the Covenant*. Phillipsburg, N.J.: Presbyterian & Reformed, 2003.

Schmemann, Alexander. *Of Water and the Spirit*. Crestwood, N.Y.: St. Vladimir's Seminary Press, 1974.

Schnackenburg, Rudolph. *Baptism in the Thought of St. Paul*. Oxford: Blackwell, 1964.

Shurden, Walter B., ed. *Proclaiming the Baptist Vision of Baptism and the Lord's Supper*. Macon, Ga.: Smith & Helwys, 1999.

Stookey, Laurence Hull. *Baptism: Christ's Act in the Church*. Nashville: Abingdon, 1982.

Thurian, Max, and Geoffrey Wainwright, eds. *Baptism and Eucharist: Ecumenical Convergence in Celebration*. Geneva: World Council of Churches, 1984.

———. *Ecumenical Perspectives on Baptism, Eucharist and Ministry*. Geneva: World Council of Churches, 1983.

Tyler, John R. *Baptism: We've Got It Right and Wrong*. Macon, Ga.: Smith & Helwys, 2003.

Vander Zee, Leonard J. *Christ, Baptism and the Lord's Supper: Recovering the Sacraments for Evangelical Worship*. Downers Grove, Ill.: InterVarsity, 2004.

Wainwright, Geoffrey. *Christian Initiation*. Cambridge: Lutterworth, 1969.

Warns, Johannes. *Baptism: Studies in Original Christian Baptism*. Minneapolis: Klock & Klock, 1980.

Watson, T. E. *Should Infants Be Baptized?* Grand Rapids: Guardian, 1962.

White, R. E. O. *The Biblical Doctrine of Initiation: A Theology of Baptism and Evangelism*. Grand Rapids: Eerdmans, 1960.

Yarnold, Edward. *The Awe Inspiring Rites of Initiation*. Collegeville, Minn.: Liturgical, 1994.

A number of ancient and modern resources exist to help churches practice the rite of baptism in public worship. Most historic denominations have their respective guides and liturgical aids. The reader can consult any of these to get an idea of how various churches practice baptism. One book designed for Protestant churches that includes helpful resources on baptism is *Baker's Worship Handbook: Traditional and Contemporary Service Resources*, Paul E. Engle (Grand Rapids: Baker, 1998).

ABOUT THE CONTRIBUTORS

John H. Armstrong, general editor, is president of ACT 3, a ministry for the advancement of the Christian tradition in the third millennium. A pastor for over twenty years, he now serves the church at-large as a teacher, apologist, and evangelist. He is an adjunct professor of evangelism at Wheaton College Graduate School and teaches as a special guest at several seminaries. He is the author/editor of a number of books, including *The Catholic Mystery*; *Roman Catholicism: Evangelical Protestants Analyze What Divides and Unites Us*; *The Stain That Stays: The Church's Response to the Sexual Misconduct of Its Leaders*; *The Glory of Christ*; and *Reforming Pastoral Ministry*. He is the editor of *ACT 3 Review*, a quarterly journal for faith, church, and culture. His reviews and articles have appeared in numerous periodicals and multi-authored works, and his online commentaries regularly appear at www.Act3online.com. He holds degrees from both Wheaton College and Wheaton Graduate School and earned the DMin degree (1979) at Luther Rice Seminary (Atlanta). He and his wife, Anita, live in Carol Stream, Illinois.

John D. Castelein is professor of contemporary Christian theology at Lincoln Christian College and Seminary in Lincoln, Illinois, where he has taught since 1977. Born in France and reared in Belgium, he became an American citizen in 1984. He received degrees from Lincoln Christian College and Lincoln Christian Seminary and earned the PhD degree from The Divinity School of the University of Chicago in 1988. He is a minister in the Christian Churches and has been both a pastor and missionary for several congregations in his church. He co-edited *Taking Every Thought Captive: Essays in Honor of James D. Strauss* and has contributed articles to several edited collections. His reviews and articles have appeared in a number of journals and periodicals. His special interests include theology in contemporary movies, spiritual formation and discipleship, and preaching in a pluralistic world and church. He and his wife, Marie, live in Lincoln, Illinois.

Robert Kolb is mission professor of systematic theology and director of the Institute for Mission Studies at Concordia Theological Seminary in St. Louis, Missouri. He received an undergraduate degree from Concordia College (Fort Wayne, Indiana) and two master's degrees from Concordia Seminary in St. Louis. He received a master's and doctorate from the University of Wisconsin. An ordained minister of the Lutheran Church - Missouri Synod (LCMS), he has served as a minister and as a professor at Concordia College (St. Paul, Minnesota), as well as a guest instructor at Luther Northwestern Theological Seminary (St. Paul, Minnesota) and Lutherische Theologische Hochschule (Oberursel, Germany). He is the author of eight books, including *Bound Choice, Election, and Wittenberg: Theological Method from Luther to the Formula of Concord*; *Confessing the Faith: Reformers Define the Church, 1530–1580*; and *For All the Saints: Changing Perceptions of Martyrdom and Sainthood in the Lutheran Reformation*. He is co-editor, with Timothy Wengert, of a translation of *The Book of Concord: The Confessions of the Evangelical Lutheran Church*. He and his wife, Pauline, live in St. Louis, Missouri.

Thomas J. Nettles is professor of church history at Southern Baptist Theological Seminary in Louisville, Kentucky. A graduate of Mississippi College, he received a master's and doctorate from Southwestern Baptist Theological Seminary. He previously taught at Trinity Evangelical Divinity School (Deerfield, Illinois), Southwestern Baptist Theological Seminary (Fort Worth, Texas), and Mid-America Baptist Theological Seminary (Memphis, Tennessee). Along with numerous journal articles and scholarly papers, he is the author or editor of nine books, including *By His Grace* and *For His Glory*. He is the coauthor of *Baptists and the Bible*, and *Why I Am a Baptist*. He and his wife, Margaret, live in Louisville, Kentucky.

Richard L. Pratt Jr. is professor of Old Testament at Reformed Theological Seminary in Orlando, Florida, and the president and founder of Third Millennium Ministries. He has taught at Reformed Seminary since 1984 and previously taught at several other schools. He holds degrees from Roanoke College (Salem, Virginia), Westminster Theological Seminary (Philadelphia, Pennsylvania), and Union Theological Seminary (Richmond, Virginia). His doctorate was received at Harvard Divinity School in 1987. An ordained minister in the Presbyterian Church in America (PCA), he has served as a pastor and Christian educator in several local churches. He is the author of six books, including biblical commentaries and *Every Thought Captive*; *Pray With Your Eyes Open*; and *Designed for Dignity*. He has also produced a number of video series, including *The Primeval History: Genesis 1–11* (Third Millennium Ministries) and *Why Do We Baptize Our Children?* (Third Millennium Ministries). He has contributed numerous articles and reviews to periodicals and dictionaries and served as a general editor of the *NIV Spirit of the Reformation Study Bible*. He and his wife, Gena, live in Casselberry, Florida.

Paul E. Engle, series editor for Counterpoints: Church Life, is an ordained minister who served for twenty-two years in pastoral ministry in Pennsylvania, Connecticut, Illinois, and Michigan. He has been an adjunct teacher in several seminaries in this country and internationally, teaching homiletics and doctor of ministry classes. He is a graduate of Houghton College (BA), Wheaton College Graduate School (MDiv), and Westminster Theological Seminary (DMin). He is the author of eight books, including *Baker's Wedding Handbook* and *Baker's Worship Handbook*. He serves as associate publisher for editorial development and executive editor at Zondervan. He and his wife, Margie, live in Grand Rapids, Michigan.

DISCUSSION AND REFLECTION QUESTIONS

CHAPTER 1: BAPTISM AS A SYMBOL OF CHRIST'S SAVING WORK

1. In examining every command, example, and implication concerning baptism in Scripture, can the reader discover any warrant for applying baptism to any but those who hear the gospel, repent of sin, and believe in Christ?
2. If circumcision came subsequent to Abraham's faith and thus subsequent to his justification and constitutes no part of his right standing before God (as Paul argues), then how, by analogy, should Christians view baptism in its relation to faith and justification?
3. If regeneration occurs at baptism, why do so many who are baptized never show the biblical marks of regeneration as set forth in 1 John 3:9 and many other Bible verses?
4. Should a church, believing that baptism precedes and involves church membership, be willing to accept an applicant for church membership who, in its view, has not been baptized?

CHAPTER 2: BAPTISM AS A SACRAMENT OF THE COVENANT

1. If "sacrament" is not a biblical term, then why is it used to describe baptism? What are the implications of the belief that the relation between baptism and grace is mysterious?
2. Why is it important to distinguish adequately between the rite of baptism and the reception of divine grace? Are there biblical examples that demonstrate this separation?

3. How can we justify drawing from patterns of OT faith to elucidate patterns of NT faith? What analogies exist between the Passover and circumcision in the OT, and the Lord's Supper and baptism in the NT?

4. What is the difference between entry and life in the visible church and in the invisible church? Why is this distinction important for understanding baptism?

5. The new covenant is predicted to be without unbelievers (Jer. 31:31–35). Why does the visible church still have baptized unbelievers within it?

6. If there are no NT passages that explicitly command or indisputably exemplify infant baptism, what implicit NT evidence is there to support the practice?

CHAPTER 3: GOD'S BAPTISMAL ACT AS REGENERATIVE

1. If Jesus really could have used other ways of describing entry into his kingdom (John 3:1–15), why, in the light of the biblical understanding of God as Creator, did he choose to describe this entry as a "new birth" or "birth from above" rather than as a commercial agreement, a romantic proposal, or some other metaphor?

2. On the basis of Paul's argument in Romans 6, how would the apostle answer someone who said, "I'm baptized. That means I am free to do anything I please! The more I sin, the more God has to forgive—and he likes to forgive!"?

3. If individual biblical teachings fit together in a "body of doctrine," then what is the relationship in Titus 3:3–8 between the "washing of rebirth and renewal" and the teachings of Paul on sin, on grace, on Christ, and on the good works of the believer?

4. If it is God who places believers together in a congregation or community of his people through baptism (1 Cor. 12:12–13), then what does that say about our relationship to our siblings in the household of God? What difference does it make for Christians that their relationship with others in the church as brothers and sisters flows from the relationship God has established with them as Father?

CHAPTER 4: BELIEVERS' BAPTISM AS THE BIBLICAL OCCASION OF SALVATION

1. Compare similarities and contrast differences between what happens at a baptism and what happens at a wedding.
2. If sinners are saved by trusting in Jesus' completed work on the cross and by repenting of their sins, what problems does this understanding present for those who baptize infants for their salvation? How would you evaluate the various solutions proposed to resolve these theological problems centered around the proper subjects of baptism?
3. What is the connection in Jesus' mind and life (and in the Christian disciple's mind and life) between being baptized and dying? Which Scriptures address these connections in the NT?
4. Fill in this table of the conversions in Acts. Indicate the appropriate verses where the specified actions are explicitly stated or clearly implied. What observations does this lead you to make concerning the conversion process in the book of Acts?

People Converted in the Book of Acts	Hearing Word	Believing, Obeying	Repenting of Sins	Being Baptized	Professing Jesus
Jews at Pentecost 2:14-41					
Jerusalem Jews 5:12-14					
Jewish priests 6:7					
Samaritans 8:4-25					
Ethiopian eunuch 8:26-40					

People Converted in the Book of Acts	Hearing Word	Believing, Obeying	Repenting of Sins	Being Baptized	Professing Jesus
Saul/Paul 9:1-19; 22:1-16; 26:1-18					
Cornelius 10:23-11:18					
In Antioch 11:19-21					
Cypriots 13:4-12					
Pisidians 13:48					
Iconians 14:1					
Lydia 16:11-15					
Jailer 16:25-34					
Thessalonians 17:4					
Bereans 17:11-13					
Athenians 17:34					
Corinthians 18:7-8					
Apollos 18:24-26					
Disciples of John 19:1-7					

SCRIPTURE INDEX

SUBJECT INDEX

Share Your Thoughts

With the Author: Your comments will be forwarded to
the author when you send them to *zauthor@zondervan.com*.

With Zondervan: Submit your review of this book
by writing to *zreview@zondervan.com*.

Free Online Resources at
www.zondervan.com

Zondervan AuthorTracker: Be notified whenever your
favorite authors publish new books, go on tour, or post
an update about what's happening in their lives.

Daily Bible Verses and Devotions: Enrich your life
with daily Bible verses or devotions that help you start
every morning focused on God.

Free Email Publications: Sign up for newsletters on
fiction, Christian living, church ministry, parenting, and
more.

Zondervan Bible Search: Find and compare
Bible passages in a variety of translations at
www.zondervanbiblesearch.com.

Other Benefits: Register yourself to receive online
benefits like coupons and special offers, or to participate
in research.

ZONDERVAN
.com